50 *Classic* CURRIES

50 *Classic* CURRIES

AUTHENTIC, DELICIOUSLY SPICY DISHES, SHOWN IN OVER 300 PHOTOGRAPHS

MANISHA KANANI

LORENZ BOOKS

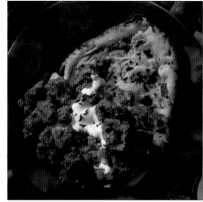

This edition is published by Lorenz Books,
an imprint of Anness Publishing Ltd,
108 Great Russell Street,
London WC1B 3NA;
info@anness.com

www.lorenzbooks.com;
www.annesspublishing.com;
twitter: @Anness_Books

If you like the images in this book and would like to investigate using them for publishing, promotions or advertising, please visit our website www.practicalpictures.com for more information.

© Anness Publishing Ltd 2015

Publisher: Joanna Lorenz
Editors: Anne Hildyard and Lucy Doncaster
Photographer: David Jordan
Food and props for styling: Judy Williams
Production Controller: Pirong Wang

AUTHOR'S ACKNOWLEDGEMENTS
I would like to thank Girish Bhogra, Ketan Natalia, Judy Williams, David Jordan and Meena Unarket, all of whom have helped in their own special way. Thank you for helping turn a dream into a reality. Above all, I would like to thank my family (especially my mum) for their patience, support and encouragement, and for tasting my numerous creations with such enthusiasm. I'm sure they've all had enough of curries for a while.

COOK'S NOTES
Bracketed terms are intended for American readers.

For all recipes, quantities are given in both metric and imperial measures and, where appropriate, in standard cups and spoons. Follow one set of measures, but not a mixture, because they are not interchangeable.

Standard spoon and cup measures are level.
1 tsp = 5ml, 1 tbsp = 15ml, 1 cup = 250ml/8fl oz.

Australian standard tablespoons are 20ml. Australian readers should use 3 tsp in place of 1 tbsp for measuring small quantities.

American pints are 16fl oz/2 cups. American readers should use 20fl oz/2.5 cups in place of 1 pint when measuring liquids.

Electric oven temperatures in this book are for conventional ovens. When using a fan oven, the temperature will probably need to be reduced by about 10–20°C/20–40°F. Since ovens vary, you should check with your manufacturer's instruction book for guidance.

Medium (US large) eggs are used unless otherwise stated.

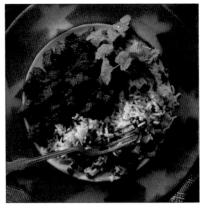

Contents

Introduction

The popularity of Indian food has continued to grow over the years and supermarkets are now selling a wide range of spices, vegetables and international ingredients. Cooking Indian food has never been easier.

There is a misconception that Indian food is time-consuming and difficult to cook. However, nothing could be further from the truth – with a basic understanding of the spices and their influences, Indian cooking can be simple.

Below: Many Indian dishes are based on just a few simple ingredients, such as rice and vegetables.

The secret of the cuisine lies in the imaginative use of spices. Different cooking techniques bring out a different flavour from each spice, and the taste combinations are endless; no wonder there is such a diverse spectrum of dishes.

There is no rigid structure to an Indian meal. Traditionally, all the dishes are served at once and the diners help themselves. A meal should have a good balance of moist and dry dishes, and bread and/or rice are nearly always served, accompanied by poppadums and a selection of pickles and chutneys.

You will find some well-known restaurant classics in this book, such as Chicken Tikka Masala and Mixed Vegetable Curry, together with some more innovative dishes, all of which illustrate the versatility of Indian cooking and will open your eyes to a new world of possibilities. There is nothing more satisfying than a curry or pilaff when it is freshly cooked at home. If you always believed that long, slow cooking methods and complicated preparations were essential to create the authentic tastes and aromas of Indian food then this book will prove to be a refreshing culinary experience – and allow you to enjoy cooking and eating in true Indian style.

Opposite: Different combinations of aromatic spices are skillfully blended in Indian cuisine to create myriad flavoursome dishes.

Spices

It is the blending of various types of spices, seasonings and flavourings that gives Indian food its character and, in some instances, its colour too.

Bay leaves
These fragrant leaves are used in many meat and rice dishes (1).

Cardamom
These small pods are green, black and creamy-beige, with green being the most common. Whole pods used in rice and meat dishes should not be eaten. Use black seeds in desserts (2).

Cayenne pepper
Sometimes called red pepper powder, this is hot or very hot, and is widely used (3).

Cinnamon
This warm spice is available whole or ground. The sticks should not be eaten (4).

Cloves
These are used in garam masala, and in meat and rice dishes (5).

Coriander
One of the most popular spices, the small beige seeds are used whole and ground. The leaves, also known as cilantro, are used for flavouring and as a garnish (6).

Cumin
Available as dark brown seeds and ground. The whole seeds are often fried in oil, releasing a musky flavour and aroma (7).

Curry leaves
These aromatic leaves are the Indian version of bay leaves (8).

Curry powder
There are many variations of this spice mixture, varying in flavour and colour (9).

Dried chillies
These red chillies are often fried in oil to release their strong flavour. The small ones are the most pungent (10).

Fennel seeds
These small light green seeds are used in many vegetable and meat dishes, and are also chewed to freshen breath (11).

Fenugreek seeds
Small, pungent seeds, these are used in spice mixtures (12).

Garam masala
This is the main spice mixture of Indian cooking. It is a hot and aromatic powder and is added at the end of cooking (13).

Garlic
Available fresh and ground, garlic is used for its strong flavour. The powder is mainly used in spice mixtures (14).

Ginger
Both fresh and ground ginger have a sharp, refreshing flavour. Fresh root ginger should be peeled before use (15).

Mint
Fresh mint leaves have a very refreshing flavour and are used in making chutneys and raitas (16).

Mustard seeds
The whole black seeds are used in some vegetable and bean dishes (17).

Nutmeg
Available whole and ground, nutmeg has a sweet, nutty flavour (18).

Paprika
A mild, sweet red powder, paprika adds colour to dishes (19).

Peppercorns
Black peppercorns are used whole and ground, and appear in garam masala (20).

Saffron
The dried stigmas of the saffron crocus, saffron is used in savoury and sweet dishes for its aroma and colour (21).

Sesame seeds
These creamy-white seeds are used in vegetable dishes and as a garnish (22).

Tamarind
The tamarind pod is dried to form a dark brown, sticky pulp that is soaked in hot water, then strained before use. It has a strong, sour taste (23).

Turmeric
This bitter yellow powder is used sparingly for its colouring properties (24).

Right: Fresh whole or ground spices form the basis of Indian cuisine.

Vegetables

Indian cooking specializes in a hundred different ways of using vegetables – put simply, they are indispensible.

Aubergine (eggplant)
Available in different varieties, the shiny purple aubergine is the most common type in Indian cooking. It has a strong flavour with a slightly bitter taste and is sometimes sprinkled with a little salt to extract some of the bitter juices (1).

Bitter melons
This long, knobbly green vegetable comes from Kenya and has a strong, bitter taste. To prepare a melon, peel the ridged skin with a sharp knife, scrape away and discard the seeds and chop the flesh (2).

Cauliflower
This versatile vegetable is very popular in Indian cooking and is often combined with other vegetables (3).

Chillies
These are small, hot members of the capsicum family. There are many types, varying in shape, size, colour, flavour and hotness. They are used extensively in Indian cooking – particularly fresh green ones. Seed them for a milder flavour (4).

Okra
These small green five-sided pods have a very distinctive taste and a slightly sticky, pulpy texture once cooked (5).

Onions
A popular root vegetable belonging to the allium family, onions have a strong flavour and aroma. Globe onions are the most commonly used variety for Indian cooking. Spring onions (scallions) are also used in some dishes to add colour and for their mild taste (6).

Bell peppers
These large hollow pods belong to the capsicum family and come in a variety of colours. Red peppers are slightly sweeter than green ones. (7).

Spinach
Available all year round, this green leafy vegetable has a mild delicate flavour. The leaves vary in size; only the large, thick ones need to be trimmed of their stalks. Spinach is a popular vegetable in Indian cuisine and it is cooked in many ways, both with meat and just with a mixture of other vegetables (8).

Corn
Having originated in America, corn is now grown all over the world. It has a delicious sweet, juicy flavour that is at its best just after picking (9).

Tomatoes
Available all year round in a variety of colours – ranging from red to orange, yellow to green – tomatoes are an essential ingredient in Indian cooking and are widely used to make all sorts of sauces, chutneys and relishes (10).

Right: The array of vegetables used in Indian cuisine provides a feast for all the senses.

Beans, Lentils and Rice

Beans and lentils play an important role in Indian cooking and are a fantastic source of protein. Rice is served with every meal in many parts of the country and appears in many guises.

Black-eyed beans (peas)
These cream-coloured peas have a black spot or 'eye'. They have a thinner skin than many other peas. When cooked, they have a creamy texture and a smoky flavour (1).

Chickpeas
These round beige-coloured beans have a strong, nutty flavour when they are cooked. As well as being used for curries, chickpeas are also ground into a flour that is widely used in many Indian dishes, such as pakoras and bhajees (2).

Channa dal
Very similar to yellow split peas but smaller in size and with a slightly sweeter taste, channa dhal is used in a variety of vegetable dishes and can also be deep-fried and mixed with Indian crisps (potato chips) and spices, such as in the popular snack Bombay mix (3, opposite).

Flageolet (small cannellini) beans
These are oval beans that are either white or pale green in colour. They have a very mild, refreshing flavour (4).

Green lentils or split peas
Also known as continental lentils, these have quite a strong flavour and retain their shape during cooking. Green lentils are extremely versatile and are used in a large number of Indian dishes (5, opposite).

Haricot (navy) beans
Small, white oval beans that come in different varieties, haricot beans are ideal for Indian cooking because not only do they retain their shape but they also absorb the flavours of spices well (6).

Kidney beans
One of the most popular beans used in Indian cooking, kidney beans are a dark red-brown and have a strong flavour (7).

Mung beans
These are small, round green beans with a slightly sweet flavour and creamy texture. When sprouted they produce the familiar beansprouts. Split mung beans are also used in Indian cooking and are cooked with rice to make a popular Gujarati dish (8).

Rice
The various types of rice used in Indian cuisine produce a different texture when cooked. Basmati rice is the most popular type eaten with Indian food. The long, slender grains have a distinctive and aromatic flavour (9, opposite).

Left: Dried beans and peas need to be soaked in water before being cooked.

Above: Fragrant basmati rice makes the ideal accompaniment to most Indian dishes.

Right: Some lentils cook down to a mush, while others retain their shape.

Wash all varieties of rice in several changes of water and allow to soak before cooking. Rice can be cooked either by the absorption method, whereby the rice is cooked in a measured amount of liquid; or by the boiling method, in which the rice is cooked in plenty of boiling water and then drained.

Yellow lentils

These dull orange-coloured split peas have a distinctive earthy flavour and are used to make dhal. Yellow lentils are available plain and in an oily variety (10).

Red split lentils

These lentils are readily available and cheap and can be used in place of yellow lentils for making dhal or for bulking out and thickening curries (11).

SOAKING AND COOKING TIPS

Most dried pulses, except lentils, need to be soaked overnight before cooking. Wash the pulses thoroughly and remove any stones and damaged beans or peas. Put into a large bowl and cover with plenty of cold water. When cooking, allow double the volume of water to pulses and boil for 10 minutes. This initial boiling period is essential to remove any harmful toxins. Drain, rinse and then cook in fresh water. The cooking time varies, depending on the type and their freshness. Pulses can be cooked in a pressure cooker to save time.

Lentils, on the whole, do not need soaking, but they should be washed in several changes of cold water before being cooked.

Breads

In some parts of India, bread is an integral part of a meal. Most traditional Indian ones are unleavened – that is, they do not contain any rising agent, and are made with ground wholemeal (whole-wheat) flour, known as chapati flour or *atta*. Some are dry-cooked on a griddle, some are fried with a little oil, others are deep-fried to make small savoury puffs. To enjoy Indian breads at their best, they should be made just before a meal and eaten hot.

Chapati

This is the staple bread of northern and central India. Chapatis or *rotis* are very thin, flat, unleavened breads made from ground wholemeal flour, water and a pinch of salt. They are cooked on a hot *tava*, which is a concave-shaped Indian griddle. Chapatis have a light texture and are fairly bland in taste, but spices added with the flour can make them more interesting. This may not be necessary, however, since they are usually used to scoop up very flavoursome curries and other spicy dishes (1).

Naan

This large, soft, tear-shaped bread is traditionally baked in a wood-fired *tandoor* oven, although it can also be grilled (broiled). Naan is normally made with a dough enriched with yogurt and leavened with yeast, and can be eaten with most meat or vegetable dishes. There are many varieties of naan, including: plain; fresh coriander (cilantro) and garlic; masala; peshwari (filled with nuts and raisins); paneer (Indian cheese); and butter naan (2).

Paratha

A paratha is similar to the chapati except that it contains ghee (clarified butter), which gives the bread a flaky texture. They are much thicker then chapatis and are shallow-fried as opposed to being dry-cooked.

Plain parathas are often eaten for lunch and go well with most vegetable dishes. Parathas can also be stuffed with various fillings, the most popular being spiced potato; the latter type are generally served on their own (3).

Poori

A small, deep-fried, puffy bread made from wholemeal flour, pooris are best eaten hot and are traditionally served for breakfast. They can be enjoyed simply plain or flavoured with spices such as cumin, turmeric and chilli powder, which are mixed into the dough. When served with a vegetable or fish curry, they make a perfect light snack or appetizer and are a common sight on the streets of India (4).

Right: From rich, soft naan to crispy fried poori, there is a bread for every occasion.

Curry Powder

There are many commercially blended curry powders available, but it is just as easy to make your own. This is a basic recipe for a mild curry powder, but you can adjust the quantity of dried red chilli you use to suit your taste.

Makes about 300ml/½ pint/1¼ cups
Whole spices
120ml/8 tbsp coriander seeds
60ml/4 tbsp cumin seeds
30ml/2 tbsp fennel seeds
30ml/2 tbsp fenugreek seeds
4 dried red chillies
5 curry leaves

Ground spices
15ml/1 tbsp cayenne pepper
15ml/1 tbsp turmeric
2.5ml/½ tsp salt

1 Dry-roast the whole spices in a heavy non-stick frying pan for 8–10 minutes, shaking the pan until the spices begin to darken and become aromatic. Cool.

2 Put the spices in a spice grinder and grind them to a fine powder. Add the remaining ground spices. Store in an airtight jar for up to four months.

Garam Masala

Garam means 'hot' and masala means 'spices' so the spices used are those that 'heat' the body, such as black peppercorns, cinnamon and cloves. Garam masala is added at the end of cooking and sprinkled over dishes as a garnish.

Makes about 90ml/6 tbsp
10 dried red chillies
3 x 2.5cm/1in cinnamon sticks
2 curry leaves
30ml/2 tbsp coriander seeds
30ml/2 tbsp cumin seeds
5ml/1 tsp black peppercorns
5ml/1 tsp cloves
5ml/1 tsp fenugreek seeds
5ml/1 tsp black mustard seeds
1.5ml/¼ tsp cayenne pepper

1 Dry-roast the chillies, cinnamon sticks and curry leaves in a large, heavy non-stick frying pan over a medium-high heat for 2 minutes, shaking the pan from side to side.

2 Add the coriander and cumin seeds, peppercorns, cloves, fenugreek and mustard seeds and dry-roast for another 8–10 minutes, shaking the pan from side to side until the spices begin to darken and release a rich aroma.

3 Allow the mixture to cool, then put the spices into a spice grinder or use a mortar and pestle and grind to a fine powder. Add the cayenne pepper, mix together and store the powder in an airtight jar for up to four months.

Curry Paste

A curry paste is a 'wet' blend of spices cooked with oil and vinegar, which helps to preserve the spices. A curry paste is a quick and convenient way of adding a mixture of spices to a dish.

Makes about 600ml/1 pint/2½ cups
120ml/8 tbsp coriander seeds
60ml/4 tbsp cumin seeds
30ml/2 tbsp fennel seeds
30ml/2 tbsp fenugreek seeds
4 dried red chillies
5 curry leaves
15ml/1 tbsp cayenne pepper
15ml/1 tbsp ground turmeric
150ml/¼ pint/⅔ cup white wine vinegar
250ml/8fl oz/1 cup oil

1 Put all the whole spices into a spice grinder or mortar and pestle and grind to a fine powder. Spoon into a bowl and add the remaining ground spices.

2 Mix all the ground spices with the vinegar and 75ml/5 tbsp water to form a thin paste. Heat the oil in a large, heavy frying pan over a medium-high heat and pour in the spice paste.

3 Stir-fry the spice paste for 10 minutes or until all the water has been absorbed. When the oil rises to the surface, the paste is cooked. Allow to cool slightly before spooning into sterilized jars.

Tikka Paste

A delicious, versatile paste that can be used in a variety of dishes, such as Chicken Tikka Masala, this is spicy with a slightly sour flavour. To preserve this and other pastes, pour some hot oil over the cooked mixture in the sterilized jar.

Makes about 475ml/16fl oz/2 cups
30ml/2 tbsp coriander seeds
30ml/2 tbsp cumin seeds
22.5ml/1½ tbsp garlic powder
30ml/2 tbsp paprika
15ml/1 tbsp garam masala
15ml/1 tbsp ground ginger
10ml/2 tsp cayenne pepper
2.5ml/½ tsp ground turmeric
15ml/1 tbsp dried mint
1.5ml/¼ tsp salt
5ml/1 tsp lemon juice
a few drops of red food colouring
a few drops of yellow food colouring
150ml/¼ pint/⅔ cup white wine vinegar
150ml/¼ pint/⅔ cup oil

1 Grind the coriander and cumin seeds to a fine powder. Spoon into a bowl and stir in the ground spices, mint, salt, lemon juice, food colourings, vinegar and 30ml/ 2 tbsp water to form a thin paste.

2 Heat the oil in a frying pan and stir-fry the paste for 10 minutes or until all the water has been absorbed and the oil rises to the surface. Allow to cool slightly before spooning into sterilized jars.

Skinning and Chopping Tomatoes

This is a very simple and quick way of preparing tomatoes for use in cooking and relishes, when the skins are not required and would spoil the texture of the finished dish.

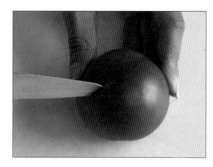

1 Using a small sharp knife, slice a cross on the bottom of each tomato, just scoring through the skin rather than cutting too deeply.

2 Put the tomatoes in a heatproof bowl and pour over boiling water. Leave for 20–30 seconds, until the skin splits. Drain and transfer to a bowl of cold water.

3 Leave the tomatoes in the cold water for about 30 seconds, then lift out of the water and peel off the skin, which should now come away easily.

Seeding and Chopping Chillies

Try using a fork to steady the chilli while you cut it with a sharp knife, to prevent your skin from coming into direct contact with the chilli. Alternatively, you could wear gloves.

1 Trim the chilli at both ends, holding the chilli still with a fork.

COOK'S TIP

If you do handle chillies, make sure you wash your hands immediately afterwards.

2 Carefully cut the chilli in half lengthwise (unless you like your food very spicy and decide not to seed it and remove the white membrane – the hottest part – in which case the chilli can be left whole and finely chopped).

3 Scrape away the seeds and the white membrane using the tip of the knife, and discard. Finely chop the flesh of the chilli, or cut it into larger pieces if you are going to add the chilli to a food processor or blender to make a paste.

Chopping Onions

One of the three key ingredients in many Indian dishes (the others being garlic and ginger), onions appear time and again in Indian recipes, so it is useful to know how to cut them quickly and easily.

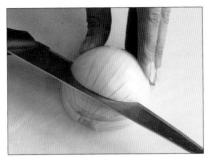

1 Trim the top off the onion, then cut it in half from root to tip, leaving the root intact. Peel off and discard the brown, papery outer skin.

2 Place the onion cut side down on a chopping board and make horizontal cuts at 5mm/¼in intervals, making sure not to cut through the root.

3 Make vertical cuts in the same way at 5mm/¼in intervals, going across the grain. Hold the onion firmly with one hand and carefully chop finely.

Preparing Fresh Ginger

Fresh ginger is very simple to prepare and adds a wonderful aromatic warmth and depth of flavour to Indian dishes. In addition to chopping ginger by hand, you can also pulp it in a food processor to create a ginger purée.

1 Break off a piece of ginger of the required length as specified in the recipe. Alternatively, you can prepare more ginger than you need for one dish and freeze the surplus. Remove and discard any rough ends.

2 Carefully peel off the brown skin using a small sharp knife or a vegetable peeler. You can also scrape off the skin using the edge of a small metal spoon if the ginger is very fresh and skin is soft enough. Discard the skin.

3 Cut the peeled ginger into thin slices and then chop it finely crossways into small pieces. Any chopped or puréed ginger you don't use can be frozen in ice cube trays and stored in the freezer for up to 2 months.

Cucumber Raita

A cool, refreshing relish, this is ideal with curries or served as a dip with dishes such as kebabs. Yogurt and other dairy products, rather than water, are the best way to counteract the heat of very spicy dishes.

Makes about 600ml/1 pint/2½ cups
½ cucumber, diced
1 green chilli, seeded and finely chopped
300ml/½ pint/1¼ cups natural
    (plain) yogurt
1.5ml/¼ tsp salt
1.5ml/¼ tsp ground cumin

VARIATIONS
• Try adding 5ml/1 tsp crushed garlic
and 15ml/1 tbsp chopped fresh mint.
• Instead of cucumber, use two skinned,
seeded and chopped tomatoes and 15ml/
1 tbsp chopped fresh coriander (cilantro).

1 Put the cucumber and chilli in a bowl. Beat the yogurt with a fork and stir everything together.

2 Stir in the salt and cumin. Cover with clear film (plastic wrap) and chill in the refrigerator until required.

Tomato and Chilli Chutney

If you like hot food, this spicy tomato chutney is the perfect accompaniment to a wide range of dishes. You can adjust the heat to suit your palate by increasing or reducing the amount of chilli you include.

Makes about 475ml/16fl oz/2 cups
4 tomatoes
1 red (bell) pepper
2 green chillies, roughly chopped
1 garlic clove, peeled and chopped
1.5ml/¼ tsp salt
2.5ml/½ tsp sugar
5ml/1 tsp cayenne pepper
45ml/3 tbsp tomato purée (paste)
15ml/1 tbsp chopped fresh coriander
    (cilantro) leaves

COOK'S TIP
This fresh chutney tastes wonderful with bread and cheese, as well as Indian dishes. Because it is not cooked, it will not keep for as long as some chutneys, and is best eaten within five days.

1 Roughly chop the tomatoes. If the skins seem coarse, you may prefer to remove them by following the technique outlined on p18. Cut the red pepper in half lengthways and remove the core, seeds and any white membrane. Roughly chop the red pepper.

2 Put all the ingredients into a blender or food processor together with 30ml/2 tbsp water and process until fairly smooth.

3 Transfer the chutney to a serving bowl, cover with clear film (plastic wrap) and chill until required.

Fresh Coriander Chutney

A popular Indian side dish, this delicious, zesty chutney is made with plenty of aromatic fresh coriander (cilantro) and is thickened with ground peanuts.

Makes about 475ml/16fl oz/2 cups
115g/4oz fresh coriander
   (cilantro) leaves
1 green chilli
2 garlic cloves
5ml/1 tsp salt
2.5ml/½ tsp sugar
22.5ml/1½ tbsp lemon juice
45ml/3 tbsp ground peanuts
120ml/4fl oz/½ cup water

VARIATIONS
• To ring the changes, you could swap half of the fresh coriander (cilantro) for fresh mint or flat leaf parsley.
• Try using fresh lime juice instead of lemon juice.

1 Roughly chop the coriander leaves using a large knife – it doesn't matter if you include a few stalks, but it is best not to use too many. Seed and roughly chop the green chilli and then peel and roughly chop the garlic cloves.

2 Put all the ingredients into a blender or food processor and process until smooth.

3 Transfer the chutney to a serving bowl, cover with clear film (plastic wrap) and chill until required.

Mint and Coconut Chutney

This mild chutney has a delicious strong flavour and an interesting texture from the coconut and sesame seeds. It would also work well with chopped fresh coriander (cilantro) or even parsley.

Makes about 350ml/12fl oz/1½ cups
50g/2oz fresh mint leaves
90ml/6 tbsp desiccated (dry unsweetened
   shredded) coconut
15ml/1 tbsp sesame seeds
1.5ml/¼ tsp salt
175ml/6fl oz/¾ cup natural
   (plain) yogurt

COOK'S TIP
This chutney can be made in advance and will keep very well, covered with clear film (plastic wrap), for up to five days in the refrigerator.

1 Roughly chop the fresh mint leaves using a large knife – it doesn't matter if you include a few stalks.

2 Put all the ingredients into a food processor or blender and process until smooth. Cover and chill.

Rogan Josh

The most popular of all lamb dishes, the meat is traditionally marinated in yogurt then cooked with spices and tomatoes, which gives this curry its rich, red appearance.

Serves 4

900g/2lb lamb fillet (tenderloin)
45ml/3 tbsp lemon juice
250ml/8fl oz/1 cup natural
　　(plain) yogurt
5ml/1 tsp salt
2 garlic cloves, peeled and crushed
2.5cm/1in piece root ginger, peeled
　　and grated
60ml/4 tbsp oil
2.5ml/½ tsp cumin seeds
2 bay leaves
4 green cardamom pods
1 onion, peeled and finely chopped
10ml/2 tsp ground coriander
10ml/2 tsp ground cumin
5ml/1 tsp chilli powder
400g/14oz can chopped tomatoes
30ml/2 tbsp tomato purée (paste)
plain rice, to serve
toasted cumin seeds and bay leaves,
　　to garnish

1 Trim away any excess fat from the meat and cut it into roughly even 2.5cm/1in cubes.

2 In a bowl, mix together the lemon juice, yogurt, salt, 1 garlic clove and the ginger. Add the lamb, cover the bowl with clear film (plastic wrap) and leave to marinate in the refrigerator overnight.

3 Heat the oil in a large frying pan and fry the cumin seeds for 2 minutes or until they begin to splutter. Add the bay leaves and cardamom pods and fry for a further 2 minutes.

4 Add the onion and remaining garlic and fry for about 5 minutes. Stir in the ground coriander, cumin and chilli powder and fry for 2 minutes.

5 Add the marinated lamb and cook for about 5 minutes, stirring occasionally.

6 Add the tomatoes, tomato purée and 150ml/¼ pint/⅔ cup water. Bring to the boil then reduce the heat. Cover and simmer for about 1–1½ hours or until the meat is tender.

7 Serve with plain rice and garnish with toasted cumin seeds and bay leaves.

COOK'S TIP
Marinating helps to tenderize as well as flavour meat, so it is worth doing even if only for a couple of hours.

Matar Keema

One of the simplest Indian dishes to make, this spicy lamb curry can also be used as a tasty filling for stuffing vegetables, such as bell peppers and large beefsteak tomatoes.

Serves 4

45ml/3 tbsp oil
1 onion, peeled and finely chopped
2 garlic cloves, peeled and crushed
2.5cm/1in piece root ginger, peeled and grated
2 green chillies, finely chopped
675g/1½lb minced (ground) lamb
5ml/1 tsp ground cumin
5ml/1 tsp ground coriander
5ml/1 tsp chilli powder
5ml/1 tsp salt
175g/6oz frozen peas, thawed
30ml/2 tbsp lemon juice
fresh coriander (cilantro), to garnish
naan and natural (plain) yogurt, to serve

1 Heat the oil in a large pan and fry the onion for about 10 minutes, stirring occasionally, until golden brown. Add the garlic, ginger and chillies and fry for 2–3 minutes, stirring frequently to prevent the garlic from burning.

2 Add the minced lamb and stir-fry for about 5 minutes.

3 Stir in the ground cumin, ground coriander, chilli powder and salt along with 300ml/½ pint/1¼ cups water. Cover the pan with a lid and simmer for about 25 minutes.

4 Add the peas and lemon juice and stir to combine. Cook the curry for a further 10 minutes, uncovered, or until the meat is tender and the peas are cooked.

5 Garnish with fresh coriander and serve with naan and yogurt.

Lamb with Apricots

Lamb is combined with apricots and traditional Indian spices to produce this rich curry with a hint of sweetness. To make yellow rice, add a strand of saffron to the cooking water.

Serves 4

900g/2lb stewing lamb
30ml/2 tbsp oil
2.5cm/1in cinnamon stick
4 green cardamom pods
1 onion, peeled and chopped
15ml/1 tbsp curry paste
5ml/1 tsp ground cumin
5ml/1 tsp ground coriander
1.5ml/¼ tsp salt
175g/6oz ready-to-eat dried apricots
350ml/12fl oz/1½ cups lamb stock
yellow rice and mango chutney, to serve
fresh coriander (cilantro), to garnish

1 Using a large sharp knife, trim away any visible fat from the meat, then cut it into 2.5cm/1in cubes.

2 Heat the oil in a large pan over a medium heat and fry the cinnamon stick and cardamoms for 2 minutes, stirring often.

3 Add the onion to the pan and fry for about 6–8 minutes, stirring often, until the onion is softened.

4 Add the curry paste to the pan and fry for 2 minutes, stirring constantly. Stir in the cumin, coriander and salt and fry for 2–3 minutes.

5 Add the meat, apricots and the stock. Cover and cook for 1–1½ hours. Serve on yellow rice with the chutney in a separate bowl. Garnish with coriander.

Beef Madras

Madras curries originate from southern India and are aromatic, robust and pungent in flavour. Here it is served with rice to which small pieces of chopped tomato have been added.

Serves 4

900g/2lb stewing beef
45ml/3 tbsp oil
1 large onion, peeled and finely chopped
4 cloves
4 green cardamom pods
2 green chillies, finely chopped
2.5cm/1in piece root ginger, peeled
   and finely chopped
2 garlic cloves, peeled and crushed
2 dried red chillies
15ml/1 tbsp curry paste
10ml/2 tsp ground coriander
5ml/1 tsp ground cumin
2.5ml/½ tsp salt
150ml/¼ pint/⅔ cup beef stock
tomato rice, to serve
fresh coriander (cilantro), to garnish

1 Remove any visible fat from the meat and cut it into 2.5cm/1in cubes.

2 Heat the oil in a large frying pan and fry the onion, cloves and cardamom pods for 5 minutes. Add the green chillies, ginger, garlic and dried chillies. Fry for 2 minutes.

3 Add the curry paste and fry for 2 minutes, stirring constantly. Add the beef and fry for 5–8 minutes, stirring frequently, until all the meat pieces are lightly browned.

4 Add the coriander, cumin, salt and stock. Cover and simmer for 1–1½ hours or until the meat is tender. Serve with tomato rice and garnish with fresh coriander.

Lamb Meatballs

In this family-friendly classic, aromatic spices are combined with minced or ground meat to produce authentic Indian-style meatballs.

Serves 4

For the meatballs
675g/1½lb minced (ground) lamb
1 green chilli, roughly chopped
1 garlic clove, peeled and chopped
2.5cm/1in piece root ginger, peeled and chopped
1.5ml/¼ tsp garam masala
1.5ml/¼ tsp salt
45ml/3 tbsp chopped fresh coriander (cilantro)

For the sauce
30ml/2 tbsp oil
2.5ml/½ tsp cumin seeds
1 onion, peeled and chopped
1 garlic clove, peeled and chopped
2.5cm/1in piece root ginger, peeled and finely chopped
5ml/1 tsp ground cumin
5ml/1 tsp ground coriander
2.5ml/½ tsp salt
2.5ml/½ tsp chilli powder
15ml/1 tbsp tomato purée (paste)
400g/14oz can chopped tomatoes
rice mixed with chopped fresh coriander (cilantro), to serve
fresh coriander sprigs, to garnish

1 To make the meatballs, process all of the ingredients in a food processor just until the mixture binds together.

2 Dampen your hands to prevent the mixture from sticking as you shape it into 16 balls. Cover and chill for 10 minutes.

3 To make the sauce, heat the oil and fry the cumin seeds until they splutter. Add the onion, garlic and ginger and fry for 5 minutes. Stir in the remaining sauce ingredients and simmer for 5 minutes.

4 Add the meatballs. Bring to the boil, cover and simmer for 25–30 minutes or until the meatballs are cooked through. Serve on coriander rice and garnish with coriander sprigs.

Beef Vindaloo

A fiery hot dish originally from Goa, a 'vindaloo' curry is made using a unique blend of hot aromatic spices and vinegar to give it a distinctive spicy flavour.

Serves 4

15ml/1 tbsp cumin seeds
4 dried red chillies
5ml/1 tsp black peppercorns
5 green cardamom pods, seeds only
5ml/1 tsp fenugreek seeds
5ml/1 tsp black mustard seeds
2.5ml/½ tsp salt
2.5ml/½ tsp demerara (raw) sugar
60ml/4 tbsp white wine vinegar
60ml/4 tbsp oil
1 large onion, peeled and finely chopped
900g/2lb stewing beef, cut into cubes
2.5cm/1in piece root ginger, peeled and
    finely chopped
1 garlic clove, peeled and crushed
10ml/2 tsp ground coriander
2.5ml/½ tsp ground turmeric
plain and yellow rice, to serve

1 Put the cumin seeds, chillies, peppercorns, cardamom seeds, fenugreek seeds and mustard seeds into a coffee grinder or use a pestle and mortar, and grind to a fine powder. Add the salt, sugar and white wine vinegar and mix to a thin paste.

2 Heat 30ml/2 tbsp of the oil in a frying pan and fry the onions for 6–8 minutes, until softened. Put the onions and the spice mixture into a food processor or blender and process to a coarse paste.

3 Heat the remaining oil in the frying pan and fry the meat cubes for about 10 minutes, until lightly browned all over. Remove the beef cubes with a slotted spoon and set aside.

4 Add the ginger and garlic to the oil remaining in the frying pan and fry for 2 minutes, stirring frequently. Stir in the ground coriander and turmeric and stir-fry for 2 minutes.

5 Add the spice and onion paste and fry for about 5 minutes.

6 Return the meat to the pan together with 300ml/½ pint/1¼ cups water. Cover and simmer for 1–1½ hours or until the meat is tender. Serve with plain and yellow rice.

COOK'S TIP
To make plain and yellow rice, infuse a pinch of saffron strands or dissolve a little ground turmeric in 15ml/1 tbsp hot water. Stir the liquid into half the cooked rice until it is uniformly yellow. Carefully mix the yellow rice into the plain rice.

Lamb Kebabs

First introduced by the Muslims, kebabs have now become a favourite Indian dish. These ones are lightly spiced and served with salad and a cooling raita.

Serves 4

For the kebabs
900g/2lb minced (ground) lamb
1 large onion, peeled and chopped
5cm/2in piece root ginger, peeled
    and chopped
2 garlic cloves, peeled and crushed
1 green chilli, finely chopped
5ml/1 tsp chilli powder
30ml/2 tbsp chopped fresh
    coriander (cilantro)
5ml/1 tsp garam masala
10ml/2 tsp ground coriander
5ml/1 tsp ground cumin
5ml/1 tsp salt
1 egg, beaten
15ml/1 tbsp natural (plain) yogurt
15ml/1 tbsp oil
mixed salad, to serve

For the raita
250ml/8fl oz/1 cup natural
    (plain) yogurt
½ cucumber, finely chopped
30ml/2 tbsp chopped fresh mint
1.5ml/¼ tsp salt

1 Put all the ingredients for the kebabs, except the yogurt and oil, into a food processor and process until the mixture binds together. Spoon into a bowl, cover and chill for 1 hour.

2 For the raita, mix together all the ingredients in a small bowl, then cover and chill for 15 minutes, or until required.

3 Preheat the grill (broiler). Divide the mixture into eight portions with lightly floured hands and mould into sausage shapes. Thread on to skewers and chill.

4 Brush the kebabs lightly with the yogurt and oil and cook under a hot grill for 8–10 minutes, turning occasionally, until brown all over. Serve with salad leaves and raita.

Balti Beef

Balti curries are cooked and served in a two-handled pan known as a *karahi* and are traditionally served with naan. If you don't have a *karahi*, you can use a wok or frying pan.

Serves 4

1 red (bell) pepper
1 green (bell) pepper
30ml/2 tbsp oil
5ml/1 tsp cumin seeds
2.5ml/½ tsp fennel seeds
1 onion, peeled and cut into thick wedges
1 garlic clove, peeled and crushed
2.5cm/1in piece root ginger, peeled
    and finely chopped
1 red chilli, finely chopped
15ml/1 tbsp curry paste
2.5ml/½ tsp salt
675g/1½lb rump (round) or fillet (beef
    tenderloin) steak, cut into thick strips
coriander (cilantro) naan, to serve

1 Seed the red and green peppers and remove the white membranes, then cut them into 2.5cm/1in chunks.

2 Heat the oil in a wok, frying pan or *karahi* and fry the cumin and fennel seeds for about 2 minutes or until they begin to splutter. Add the onion, garlic, ginger and chilli and fry for 5 minutes.

3 Add the curry paste and salt and fry for a further 3–4 minutes, stirring frequently to prevent the paste from sticking to the pan and burning.

4 Add the peppers; stir-fry for 5 minutes. Stir in the beef and continue to fry for 10–12 minutes, or until the meat is tender. Serve with warm coriander naan.

Spicy Lamb and Potato Stew

This simple dish of meat and potatoes is transformed into a tasty and exciting stew with the addition of carefully selected and blended Indian spices.

Serves 4

675g/1½lb lamb fillet (tenderloin)
45ml/3 tbsp oil
1 onion, peeled and finely chopped
2 bay leaves
1 green chilli, seeded and finely chopped
2 garlic cloves, peeled and finely chopped
10ml/2 tsp ground coriander
5ml/1 tsp ground cumin
2.5ml/½ tsp ground turmeric
2.5ml/½ tsp chilli powder
2.5ml/½ tsp salt
225g/8oz tomatoes, skinned and chopped
600ml/1 pint/2½ cups lamb stock
2 large potatoes, peeled and cut into
    2.5cm/1in chunks
chopped fresh coriander (cilantro),
    to garnish
chapatis, to serve

1 Remove any visible fat from the meat and cut it into 2.5cm/1in cubes.

2 Heat the oil in a large pan and fry the onion, bay leaves, chilli and garlic for 5 minutes.

3 Add the meat and cook for 6–8 minutes, until lightly browned.

4 Add the ground coriander, cumin, turmeric, chilli powder and salt and cook for 3–4 minutes, stirring all the time to prevent the spices from sticking.

5 Add the tomatoes and stock and stir to combine. Simmer for 5 minutes, until the sauce thickens. Bring to the boil, cover the pan with a lid and leave it to simmer for 1 hour.

6 Add the potatoes and cook for a further 30–40 minutes or until the meat is tender and the potatoes are cooked.

7 Garnish with chopped fresh coriander and serve with chapatis.

VARIATION
You could use beef fillet (tenderloin) in place of the lamb, if you like.

Chicken Tikka Masala

A restaurant favourite in the West, this dish consists of tender chicken pieces cooked in a creamy, spicy tomato sauce and served on naan.

Serves 4

675g/1½lb chicken breast fillets, skinned
90ml/6 tbsp tikka paste
60ml/4 tbsp natural (plain) yogurt
30ml/2 tbsp oil
1 onion, peeled and chopped
1 garlic clove, peeled and crushed
1 green chilli, seeded and chopped
2.5cm/1in piece root ginger, peeled
    and grated
15ml/1 tbsp tomato purée (paste)
15ml/1 tbsp ground almonds
250ml/8fl oz/1 cup water
45ml/3 tbsp butter, melted
50ml/2fl oz/¼ cup double (heavy) cream
15ml/1 tbsp lemon juice
fresh coriander (cilantro) sprigs, natural
    yogurt and toasted cumin seeds,
    to garnish
naan, to serve

1 Cut the chicken into 2.5cm/1in cubes. Put 45ml/3 tbsp of the tikka paste and all of the yogurt into a bowl. Add the chicken, cover the bowl with clear film (plastic wrap) and leave to marinate for 20 minutes.

2 For the tikka sauce, heat the oil in a large pan and fry the onion, garlic, chilli and ginger for 5 minutes. Add the remaining tikka paste and fry for 2 minutes. Add the tomato purée, almonds and water, stir to combine and simmer for 15 minutes.

3 Thread the marinated chicken pieces on to wooden kebab skewers. Preheat the grill (broiler).

COOK'S TIP
Soak the wooden skewers in cold water before using to prevent them from burning while grilling (broiling).

4 Brush the chicken pieces with the butter and grill (broil) under a medium heat for 15 minutes, turning occasionally.

5 Put the tikka sauce into a food processor or blender and process until smooth. Return to the pan.

6 Stir the cream and lemon juice into the sauce in the pan. Remove the chicken pieces from the skewers and add them to the pan, then simmer for 5 minutes.

7 Serve the chicken on naan, garnished with fresh coriander, yogurt and toasted cumin seeds.

Tandoori Chicken

This classic Indian dish is traditionally cooked in the *tandoor*, which is a vat-shaped clay oven that is heated with charcoal or wood. It can also be made in a standard oven at home.

Serves 4

8 chicken pieces, such as thighs, drumsticks,
    and halved breast fillets, skinned
60ml/4 tbsp lemon juice
5ml/1 tsp salt
2 garlic cloves, peeled and chopped
2.5cm/1in piece root ginger, peeled and
    roughly chopped
2 green chillies, roughly chopped
175ml/6fl oz/¾ cup natural (plain) yogurt
5ml/1 tsp salt
5ml/1 tsp chilli powder
5ml/1 tsp garam masala
5ml/1 tsp ground cumin
5ml/1 tsp ground coriander
red food colouring (optional)
30ml/2 tbsp butter, melted
lemon wedges, to garnish
chilli powder and a sprig of fresh mint,
    to garnish
salad and Cucumber Raita (see page 20),
    to serve

1 Cut slashes in the chicken. Combine the lemon juice and the salt and rub it over the chicken. Marinate for 10 minutes.

2 Put the garlic, ginger and chillies into a food processor or blender and process until a fairly smooth paste forms. Add the mixture to a small bowl containing the natural yogurt, salt, chilli powder, garam masala, ground cumin and ground coriander, and mix well to combine everything thoroughly.

3 Brush the chicken pieces with food colouring, if using, and put into a dish. Add the marinade and chill overnight. Preheat the oven to 220°C/425°F/Gas 7. Put the chicken in a roasting pan and bake for 40 minutes, basting with butter. Serve with lemon, salad and Cucumber Raita, garnished with chilli powder and mint.

Chicken Jalfrezi

A Jalfrezi curry is a stir-fried dish cooked with onions, ginger and garlic in a rich bell pepper sauce. This one includes tender chunks of chicken and is finished with fresh herb sprigs.

Serves 4

675g/1½lb chicken breast fillets, skinned
30ml/2 tbsp oil
5ml/1 tsp cumin seeds
1 onion, peeled and finely chopped
1 green (bell) pepper, finely chopped
1 red (bell) pepper, finely chopped
1 garlic clove, peeled and crushed
2cm/¾in piece root ginger, peeled and
    finely chopped
15ml/1 tbsp curry paste
1.5ml/¼ tsp chilli powder
5ml/1 tsp ground coriander
5ml/1 tsp ground cumin
2.5ml/½ tsp salt
400g/14oz can chopped tomatoes
30ml/2 tbsp chopped fresh coriander
    (cilantro), plus a sprig, to garnish
plain rice, to serve

1 Remove any visible fat from the chicken and cut it into 2.5cm/1in cubes.

2 Heat the oil in a wok and fry the cumin seeds for 2 minutes. Add the onion, peppers, garlic and ginger. Fry for 6–8 minutes.

3 Add the curry paste to the frying pan and fry for about 2 minutes. Stir in the chilli powder, ground coriander, cumin and salt and add 15ml/1 tbsp water; fry for a further 2 minutes.

4 Add the chicken and fry for 5 minutes. Stir in the tomatoes and fresh coriander. Cover and cook for about 15 minutes or until the chicken is tender. Serve with rice; garnish with coriander.

Chicken Korma

A korma is a rich, creamy Moghulai dish that originates from northern India. This recipe uses a combination of yogurt and cream, which gives the sauce a rich flavour.

Serves 4

675g/1½lb chicken breast fillets, skinned
25g/1oz blanched almonds
2 garlic cloves, peeled and crushed
2.5cm/1in piece root ginger, peeled
    and roughly chopped
30ml/2 tbsp oil
3 green cardamom pods
1 onion, peeled and finely chopped
10ml/2 tsp ground cumin
1.5ml/¼ tsp salt
150ml/¼ pint/⅔ cup natural
    (plain) yogurt
175ml/6fl oz/¾ cup single
    (light) cream
toasted flaked (sliced) almonds and a fresh
    coriander (cilantro) sprig, to garnish
plain rice, to serve

1 Cut the chicken breast fillets into 2.5cm/1in cubes.

2 Put the blanched almonds, garlic and ginger into a food processor or blender with 30ml/2 tbsp water and process to a smooth paste.

3 Heat the oil in a large frying pan and cook the chicken for 8–10 minutes or until it is browned all over. Remove with a slotted spoon and set aside.

4 Add the cardamom pods to the pan and fry for 2 minutes. Add the onion and fry for a further 5 minutes.

5 Stir in the almond and garlic paste, cumin and salt and cook, stirring, for a further 5 minutes.

6 Add the yogurt, a tablespoonful at a time, and cook over a low heat, until it has all been absorbed. Return the chicken to the pan. Cover and simmer over a low heat for 5–6 minutes or until the chicken is tender.

7 Add the cream and simmer for a further 5 minutes.

8 Serve with plain rice and garnish with toasted flaked almonds and coriander.

Coconut Chicken

This Goan-style curry is made from a delicious blend of authentic Indian spices and toasted coconut, which lends texture as well as flavour to the dish.

Serves 4

75g/3oz/1½ cups desiccated (dry unsweetened shredded) coconut
30ml/2 tbsp oil
2.5ml/½ tsp cumin seeds
4 black peppercorns
15ml/1 tbsp fennel seeds
15ml/1 tbsp coriander seeds
2 onions, peeled and finely chopped
2.5ml/½ tsp salt
8 small chicken pieces, such as thighs and drumsticks, skinned
fresh coriander (cilantro) sprigs and lemon wedges, to garnish
Mint and Coconut Chutney (see page 21), to serve

1 Put the coconut in a bowl with 45ml/ 3 tbsp water. Leave to soak for 15 minutes.

2 Meanwhile, heat 15ml/1 tbsp of the oil in a large frying pan. Add the cumin seeds, peppercorns, fennel seeds and coriander seeds. Fry, stirring frequently, over a low heat for 3–4 minutes, until the seeds begin to splutter.

3 Add the finely chopped onion and fry for 6–8 minutes, until softened.

4 Stir in the rehydrated desiccated coconut and salt and continue to fry for a further 5 minutes, stirring occasionally to prevent the mixture from sticking to the pan.

COOK'S TIPS

• Make the spiced coconut mixture the day before and chill it in the refrigerator, then continue from the final step when required.
• It is important to soak the coconut before adding it, or it will be too dry to be processed to a coarse paste.

5 Put the coconut mixture into a food processor or blender and process to form a coarse paste. Spoon into a bowl and set aside until required.

6 Heat the remaining oil in the frying pan and fry the chicken for 10 minutes. Stir in the coconut paste and cook over a low heat, stirring often, for 15–20 minutes or until the coconut mixture is golden brown and the chicken is tender and fully cooked through.

7 Transfer to a serving dish, garnish with fresh coriander and lemon wedges and serve with Mint and Coconut Chutney.

Chicken Dhansak

Dhansak curries originate from the Parsee community. They are traditionally made with lentils and mutton, but in this version green lentils are combined with chicken.

Serves 4

75g/3oz/½ cup green lentils
475ml/16fl oz/2 cups stock
45ml/3 tbsp oil
5ml/1 tsp cumin seeds
2 curry leaves
1 onion, peeled and finely chopped
2.5cm/1in piece root ginger, peeled
    and finely chopped
1 green chilli, finely chopped
5ml/1 tsp ground cumin
5ml/1 tsp ground coriander
1.5ml/¼ tsp salt
1.5ml/¼ tsp chilli powder
400g/14oz can chopped tomatoes
8 chicken pieces, skinned
60ml/4 tbsp chopped fresh
    coriander (cilantro)
5ml/1 tsp garam masala
fresh coriander sprigs, to garnish
plain rice, to serve

1 Rinse the lentils under cold running water. Put into a large, heavy pan with the stock. Bring to the boil, cover and simmer for about 15–20 minutes. Drain and set aside.

2 Heat the oil in a large pan and stir-fry the cumin seeds and curry leaves for 2 minutes, until the seeds pop.

3 Add the onion, ginger and chilli and fry for about 5 minutes. Stir in the cumin, coriander, salt and chilli powder with 30ml/2 tbsp water.

4 Add the chopped tomatoes and the chicken to the pan and stir to combine thoroughly. Cover the pan and cook for 10–15 minutes.

5 Add the lentils and stock, fresh coriander and garam masala. Cook for 10 minutes, until the chicken is tender. Garnish with coriander sprigs. Serve with plain rice.

Hot Chilli Chicken

Not for the faint-hearted, this fiery, hot curry is made with a spicy chilli masala paste. The best way to counteract heat is to serve fiery dishes with yogurt, as here, or a glass of milk.

Serves 4

30ml/2 tbsp tomato purée (paste)
2 garlic cloves, peeled and chopped
2 green chillies, roughly chopped
5 dried red chillies
2.5ml/$\frac{1}{2}$ tsp salt
1.5ml/$\frac{1}{4}$ tsp sugar
5ml/1 tsp chilli powder
2.5ml/$\frac{1}{2}$ tsp paprika
15ml/1 tbsp curry paste
30ml/2 tbsp oil
2.5ml/$\frac{1}{2}$ tsp cumin seeds
1 onion, peeled and finely chopped
2 bay leaves
5ml/1 tsp ground coriander
5ml/1 tsp ground cumin
1.5ml/$\frac{1}{4}$ tsp ground turmeric
400g/14oz can chopped tomatoes
150ml/$\frac{1}{4}$ pint/$\frac{2}{3}$ cup water
8 chicken thighs, skinned
5ml/1 tsp garam masala
sliced green chillies, to garnish
chapatis and natural (plain) yogurt,
    to serve

1 Put the tomato purée, garlic, green and dried red chillies, salt, sugar, chilli powder, paprika and curry paste into a food processor or blender and process to a smooth paste.

2 Heat the oil in a large pan and fry the cumin seeds for 2 minutes, stirring often, until they pop. Add the onion and the bay leaves and fry for about 5 minutes, until the onion is softened slightly.

3 Add the chilli paste. Fry for 2–3 minutes. Add the remaining ground spices and cook for 2 minutes. Add the tomatoes and water, bring to the boil and simmer for 5 minutes, until the sauce thickens.

4 Add the chicken and garam masala. Cover and simmer for 25–30 minutes, until the chicken is tender. Serve with chapatis and natural yogurt, garnished with sliced green chillies.

Chicken Saag

A mildly spiced dish using a popular combination of spinach and chicken, this recipe is best made using fresh spinach, but if this is unavailable you can use the frozen type instead.

Serves 4

225g/8oz fresh spinach leaves, washed but not dried
2.5cm/1in piece root ginger, peeled and grated
2 garlic cloves, crushed
1 green chilli, roughly chopped
200ml/7fl oz/ scant 1 cup water
30ml/2 tbsp oil
2 bay leaves
1.5ml/¼ tsp black peppercorns
1 onion, peeled and finely chopped
4 tomatoes, skinned and finely chopped
10ml/2 tsp curry powder
5ml/1 tsp salt
5ml/1 tsp chilli powder
45ml/3 tbsp natural (plain) yogurt
8 chicken thighs, skinned
natural yogurt and chilli powder, to garnish
masala naan, to serve

1 Cook the spinach, without water, in a tightly covered pan for 5 minutes. Purée the spinach, ginger, garlic, chilli and 50ml/2fl oz/¼ cup of the water in a food processor or blender.

2 Heat the oil in a large pan, add the bay leaves and black peppercorns and fry for 2 minutes, stirring frequently. Add the finely chopped onion and fry for 6–8 minutes or until the onion has browned and softened.

3 Add the skinned, chopped tomatoes to the pan and simmer for about 5 minutes. Stir in the curry powder, salt and chilli powder and cook for about 2 minutes, stirring frequently.

4 Add the spinach purée and 150ml/¼ pint/⅔ cup water to the pan. Stir to combine well, then simmer for 5 minutes, stirring frequently.

5 Add the yogurt, 15ml/1 tbsp at a time and simmer for 5 minutes.

6 Add the chicken. Cover and cook for 25–30 minutes or until the chicken is tender. Serve on masala naan, drizzle over some natural yogurt and dust lightly with chilli powder.

Jeera Chicken

An aromatic dish with a distinctive taste of cumin, this is best served simply with a salad and yogurt, although you could serve it with some bread for a more substantial meal.

Serves 4

45ml/3 tbsp cumin seeds
45ml/3 tbsp oil
2.5ml/½ tsp black peppercorns
4 green cardamom pods
2 green chillies, finely chopped
2 garlic cloves, peeled and crushed
2.5cm/1in piece root ginger, peeled
    and grated
5ml/1 tsp ground coriander
10ml/2 tsp ground cumin
2.5ml/½ tsp salt
8 chicken pieces, such as thighs and
    drumsticks, skinned
5ml/1 tsp garam masala
fresh coriander (cilantro) and chilli
    powder, to garnish
Cucumber Raita (see page 20), to serve

1 Dry-roast 15ml/1 tbsp of the cumin seeds in a pan for 5 minutes. Set aside.

2 Heat the oil in a large pan and fry the remaining cumin seeds, black peppercorns and cardamoms for about 2–3 minutes, until they sputter.

3 Add the chillies, garlic and ginger and fry for 2 minutes, stirring frequently.

4 Add the coriander, cumin and salt and cook for 2–3 minutes, stirring often.

5 Add the chicken pieces and turn them to coat them in the spice mixture. Cover the pan with a lid or plate and simmer for 20–25 minutes.

6 Add the garam masala and reserved toasted cumin seeds and cook for a further 5 minutes, until the chicken is tender and completely cooked through. Serve with Cucumber Raita, garnished with chilli powder and fresh coriander.

VARIATION
Although not authentic, this dish would also work well with duck pieces in place of the chicken.

Balti Chicken Curry

In this colourful dish, tender pieces of chicken are lightly cooked with fresh vegetables and aromatic spices in the traditional Balti style.

Serves 4

675g/1½lb chicken breast fillets, skinned
30ml/2 tbsp oil
2.5ml/½ tsp cumin seeds
2.5ml/½ tsp fennel seeds
1 onion, peeled and thickly sliced
2 garlic cloves, peeled and crushed
2.5cm/1in piece root ginger, peeled
    and finely chopped
15ml/1 tbsp curry paste
225g/8oz broccoli, broken into florets
4 tomatoes, cut into thick wedges
5ml/1 tsp garam masala
30ml/2 tbsp chopped fresh
    coriander (cilantro)
naan, to serve

1 Remove any fat and cut the chicken into 2.5cm/1in cubes.

2 Heat the oil in a wok and fry the cumin and fennel seeds for 2 minutes until the seeds begin to splutter. Add the onion, garlic and ginger and cook for 5–7 minutes. Stir in the curry paste and cook for a further 2–3 minutes.

3 Add the broccoli florets to the pan and fry for about 5 minutes, stirring often. Add the chicken cubes and stir-fry for 5–8 minutes.

4 Add the tomatoes, garam masala and chopped coriander. Cook for a further 5–10 minutes or until the chicken is tender. Serve with naan.

Chicken Dopiazza

Dopiazza literally translates as 'two onions'. In this chicken dish, two types of onions are used at different stages during the cooking process, resulting in different textures.

Serves 4

45ml/3 tbsp oil
8 small onions, peeled and halved
2 bay leaves
8 green cardamom pods
4 cloves
3 dried red chillies
8 black peppercorns
2 onions, peeled and finely chopped
2 garlic cloves, peeled and crushed
2.5cm/1in piece root ginger, peeled
    and finely chopped
5ml/1 tsp ground coriander
5ml/1 tsp ground cumin
2.5ml/½ tsp ground turmeric
5ml/1 tsp chilli powder
2.5ml/½ tsp salt
4 tomatoes, skinned and finely chopped
120ml/4fl oz/½ cup water
8 chicken pieces, such as thighs and
    drumsticks, skinned
plain rice, to serve

1 Heat 30ml/2 tbsp of the oil in a large pan and fry the halved small onions for 10 minutes, or until golden brown. Remove with a slotted spoon and set aside on kitchen paper.

2 Add the remaining oil and fry the bay leaves, cardamoms, cloves, chillies and peppercorns for 2 minutes.

3 Add the chopped onions, garlic and ginger and fry for 5 minutes. Stir in the ground spices and salt; cook for 2 minutes.

4 Add the tomatoes and the water and simmer for 5 minutes until the sauce thickens. Add the chicken and cook for about 15 minutes.

5 Add the reserved small onions, then cover and cook for a further 10 minutes, or until the chicken is tender. Serve with plain rice.

Prawn Curry

A rich, flavoursome curry made from prawns or shrimp and a delicious blend of aromatic spices, this dish is quick and easy to put together and tastes wonderful.

Serves 4

675g/1½lb raw tiger prawns (shrimp)
4 dried red chillies
50g/2oz/1 cup desiccated (dry
    unsweetened shredded) coconut
5ml/1 tsp black mustard seeds
1 large onion, peeled and chopped
45ml/3 tbsp oil
4 bay leaves
2.5cm/1in piece root ginger, peeled
    and finely chopped
2 garlic cloves, peeled and crushed
15ml/1 tbsp ground coriander
5ml/1 tsp chilli powder
5ml/1 tsp salt
4 tomatoes, finely chopped
plain rice, to serve

1 Peel the prawns, then make a cut along the back of each one and remove the vein.

2 Put the dried red chillies, coconut, mustard seeds and onion in a large frying pan and dry-fry for 8–10 minutes, until the mixture begins to brown. Process to a coarse paste in a food processor or blender.

3 Heat the oil in the frying pan and fry the bay leaves for 1 minute. Add the chopped ginger and the garlic and fry for 2–3 minutes, stirring frequently.

4 Add the coriander, chilli powder, salt and the paste and fry for 5 minutes.

5 Stir in the tomatoes and 175ml/6fl oz/ ¾ cup water and simmer for 5–6 minutes or until thickened.

6 Add the prawns to the pan and cook for about 4–5 minutes or until they turn pink and the edges are curling slightly. Take care not to overcook the prawns. Serve with plain rice.

COOK'S TIP
Serve some extra cooked tiger prawns (shrimp), unpeeled, on the edge of each plate for an attractive garnish. Cook them at the same time as the peeled prawns in the frying pan.

Green Fish Curry

This creamy curry is fairly mild but has a complex flavour thanks to the careful blend of spices used. Cod is traditional, but you may prefer to use a more sustainable type of white fish.

Serves 4

1.5ml/¼ tsp ground turmeric
30ml/2 tbsp lime juice
pinch of salt
4 cod fillets, skinned and cut into
    5cm/2in chunks
1 onion, peeled and chopped
1 green chilli, roughly chopped
1 garlic clove, peeled and grated
25g/1oz/¼ cup cashew nuts
2.5ml/½ tsp fennel seeds
30ml/2 tbsp desiccated (dry unsweetened
    shredded) coconut
30ml/2 tbsp oil
1.5ml/¼ tsp cumin seeds
1.5ml/¼ tsp ground coriander
1.5ml/¼ tsp ground cumin
1.5ml/¼ tsp salt
150ml/¼ pint/⅔ cup water
175ml/6fl oz/¾ cup single (light) cream
45ml/3 tbsp finely chopped fresh
    coriander (cilantro), plus a sprig,
    to garnish
Vegetable Pilau (see page 94), to serve

1 Mix together the turmeric, lime juice and salt in a small bowl and rub the mixture over the fish. Cover with clear film (plastic wrap) and leave to marinate for 15 minutes.

2 Meanwhile process the onion, chilli, garlic, cashew nuts, fennel seeds and coconut to a paste in a food processor or with a mortar and pestle. Spoon the paste into a bowl and set aside.

3 Heat the oil in a large frying pan and fry the cumin seeds for 2 minutes until they begin to splutter. Add the paste and fry for 5 minutes, then stir in the ground coriander, cumin, salt and water and fry for about 2–3 minutes.

4 Add the cream and the fresh coriander. Simmer for 5 minutes. Add the fish and gently stir in. Cover and cook gently for 10 minutes, until the fish is tender. Serve with Vegetable Pilau, garnished with a coriander sprig.

Indian Fish Stew

A spicy fish stew made with potatoes, peppers and traditional Indian spices, this delicious dish can be served on its own or with chapatis to scoop up the sauce.

Serves 4

30ml/2 tbsp oil
5ml/1 tsp cumin seeds
1 onion, peeled and chopped
1 red (bell) pepper, thinly sliced
1 garlic clove, peeled and crushed
2 red chillies, finely chopped
2 bay leaves
2.5ml/½ tsp salt
5ml/1 tsp ground cumin
5ml/1 tsp ground coriander
5ml/1 tsp chilli powder
400g/14oz can chopped tomatoes
2 large potatoes, peeled and cut into
   2.5cm/1in chunks
300ml/½ pint/1¼ cups fish stock
4 white fish fillets
chapatis, to serve

1 Heat the oil in a large, deep-sided frying pan and fry the cumin seeds for 2 minutes until they begin to splutter. Add the onion, pepper, garlic, chillies and bay leaves and fry for 5–7 minutes until the onions have browned.

2 Add the salt, ground cumin, ground coriander and chilli powder and cook for 3–4 minutes.

COOK'S TIP
Good, sustainable types of white fish for this and other dishes may include coley, pollack or gurnard, but it is best to check which species are recommended for the area in which you live.

3 Stir in the tomatoes, potatoes and fish stock. Bring to the boil and simmer for a further 10 minutes.

4 Add the fish, then cover and simmer for 10 minutes, or until the fish is tender. Serve with chapatis.

Tuna Fish Curry

This unusual fish curry, made from canned tuna, can be put together in minutes using mostly storecupboard or pantry ingredients. You could also use canned salmon.

Serves 4

45ml/3 tbsp oil
1.5ml/¼ tsp cumin seeds
2.5ml/½ tsp ground cumin
2.5ml/½ tsp ground coriander
2.5ml/½ tsp chilli powder
1.5ml/¼ tsp salt
2 garlic cloves, crushed
1 onion, peeled and thinly sliced
1 red (bell) pepper, seeded and
    thinly sliced
1 green (bell) pepper, seeded and
    thinly sliced
400g/14oz can tuna, drained
1 green chilli, finely chopped
2.5cm/1in piece root ginger, peeled
    and grated
1.5ml/¼ tsp garam masala
5ml/1 tsp lemon juice
30ml/2 tbsp chopped fresh coriander
    (cilantro), plus a sprig, to garnish
pitta and Cucumber Raita (see page 20),
    to serve

1 Heat the oil in a large frying pan and fry the cumin seeds for 2 minutes.

2 Add the cumin, coriander, chilli powder and salt; cook for 2–3 minutes. Add the garlic, onion and peppers.

3 Fry the vegetables, stirring from time to time, for 5–7 minutes, until the onions have browned.

4 Stir in the tuna, chilli and ginger and cook for 5 minutes.

5 Add the garam masala, lemon juice and fresh coriander and continue to cook for a further 3–4 minutes. Serve in warmed, split pitta with the Cucumber Raita garnished with a coriander sprig.

COOK'S TIP
Place the pitta on a grill (broiler) rack and grill for about 30 seconds, until it just puffs up. It will then be easy to split down the side with a sharp knife. Take care, as steam will escape when you make the cut.

Goan-style Mussels

Mussels are best cooked simply, and here they are allowed to shine in a dish that uses just a few aromatic ingredients that complement the mussels' flavour.

Serves 4

900g/2lb live mussels
115g/4oz creamed coconut or 450ml/
    ³⁄₄ pint/1³⁄₄ cups coconut cream
45ml/3 tbsp oil
1 onion, peeled and finely chopped
3 garlic cloves, peeled and crushed
2.5cm/1in piece root ginger, peeled and
    finely chopped
2.5ml/¹⁄₂ tsp ground turmeric
5ml/1 tsp ground cumin
5ml/1 tsp ground coriander
1.5ml/¹⁄₄ tsp salt
chopped fresh coriander (cilantro)

1 Scrub the mussels under cold running water and remove the beards using a sharp knife. Discard any mussels that are already open.

2 Dissolve the creamed coconut, if using, in 450ml/³⁄₄ pint/1³⁄₄ cups boiling water and set aside until needed.

3 Heat the oil in a large pan and fry the onion for 5 minutes. Add the garlic and ginger and fry for 2 minutes. Stir in the turmeric, cumin, coriander and salt and fry for 2 minutes. Add the dissolved creamed coconut or the coconut cream, bring to the boil and simmer for 5 minutes.

4 Add the mussels, cover and cook for 6–8 minutes or until all the mussels are cooked and open. Spoon the mussels on to a serving platter and pour the sauce over, then top with the fresh coriander.

Coconut Salmon

Meaty salmon steaks are the ideal platform for showcasing a blend of spices and aromatic ingredients. Here, they are cooked in a creamy, subtly spiced sauce.

Serves 4

10ml/2 tsp ground cumin
10ml/2 tsp chilli powder
2.5ml/½ tsp ground turmeric
30ml/2 tbsp white wine vinegar
1.5ml/¼ tsp salt
4 salmon steaks, about 175g/6oz each
45ml/3 tbsp oil
1 onion, peeled and chopped
2 green chillies, seeded and chopped
2 garlic cloves, peeled and crushed
2.5cm/1in piece root ginger, peeled
    and grated
5ml/1 tsp ground coriander
175ml/6fl oz/¾ cup coconut milk
spring onion (scallion) rice, to serve
fresh coriander (cilantro) sprigs, to garnish

COOK'S TIPS
• If coconut milk is unavailable, dissolve some grated creamed coconut in boiling water and strain it into a bowl.
• To make spring onion (scallion) rice, simply cook some rice as usual and then stir through some chopped spring onions.

1 Mix 5ml/1 tsp of the ground cumin with the chilli powder, turmeric, vinegar and salt. Rub over the salmon steaks, cover and leave to marinate for 15 minutes.

2 Heat the oil in a large, deep-sided frying pan and fry the onion, chillies, garlic and ginger for 5–6 minutes. Transfer the mixture to a food processor or blender and process to a paste.

3 Return the paste to the pan. Add the remaining cumin, coriander and coconut milk. Bring to the boil and simmer for about 5 minutes.

4 Add the salmon steaks. Cover the pan and cook for 15 minutes, until the fish is tender and cooked. Serve with spring onion rice and garnish with coriander.

Fish and Okra Curry

An interesting combination of flavours and textures is used to make this wonderful fish dish. Okra are widely used in Indian cooking, but you could use green beans if you prefer.

Serves 4

450g/1lb monkfish
5ml/1 tsp ground turmeric
2.5ml/½ tsp chilli powder
2.5ml/½ tsp salt
5ml/1 tsp cumin seeds
2.5ml/½ tsp fennel seeds
2 dried red chillies
45ml/3 tbsp oil
1 onion, peeled and finely chopped
2 garlic cloves, peeled and crushed
4 tomatoes, skinned and finely chopped
150ml/¼ pint/⅔ cup water
225g/8oz okra, trimmed and cut into
    2.5cm/1in lengths
5ml/1 tsp garam masala
tomato rice, to serve

VARIATION
Yellow and plain rice would also go well with this curry, making an attractive presentation. You could also serve it with plain rice, if you prefer.

1 Remove the membrane and bones from the monkfish, cut it into 2.5cm/1in cubes and place it in a dish. Mix together the turmeric, chilli powder and 1.5ml/¼ tsp of the salt and rub the mixture all over the fish. Marinate for 15 minutes.

2 Put the cumin seeds, fennel seeds and chillies in a large frying pan and dry-roast for 3–4 minutes. Transfer them to a blender or use a mortar and pestle to grind to a coarse powder.

3 Heat 30ml/2 tbsp of the oil in the frying pan and and fry the fish for about 4–5 minutes, stirring occasionally and being careful not to break up the fish too much. Remove with a slotted spoon and drain on kitchen paper.

4 Add the remaining oil to the frying pan and fry the onion and garlic for about 5 minutes, stirring frequently, until they are starting to soften.

5 Add the spice powder and remaining salt and fry for 2–3 minutes, stirring frequently. Stir in the tomatoes and water and simmer for 5 minutes.

6 Add the prepared okra and cook for about 5–7 minutes.

7 Return the fish to the pan together with the garam masala. Cover and simmer for 5–6 minutes or until the fish is tender. Serve with tomato rice.

Aloo Gobi

Cauliflower and potatoes are encrusted with Indian spices in this recipe, which can be served with tomato salad and pickle as a light meal, or as an accompaniment to other dishes.

3 Add the cauliflower florets and fry, stirring, for 5 minutes.

Serves 4

450g/1lb potatoes, peeled and cut into
    2.5cm/1in chunks
30ml/2 tbsp oil
5ml/1 tsp cumin seeds
1 green chilli, finely chopped
450g/1lb cauliflower, broken into florets
5ml/1 tsp ground coriander
5ml/1 tsp ground cumin
1.5ml/$\frac{1}{4}$ tsp chilli powder
2.5ml/$\frac{1}{2}$ tsp ground turmeric
2.5ml/$\frac{1}{2}$ tsp salt
chopped fresh coriander (cilantro),
    to garnish
tomato and onion salad and pickle,
    to serve

1 Par-boil the potatoes in a large pan of boiling water for 10 minutes. Drain well and set aside.

2 Heat the oil in a large frying pan and fry the cumin seeds for 2 minutes. Add the chilli and fry for a further 1 minute.

4 Add the potatoes, ground spices and salt to the pan and cook for a further 7–10 minutes, stirring occasionally, until all of the vegetables are tender and cooked through.

5 Garnish with fresh coriander and serve with tomato and onion salad and pickle.

VARIATION
You could try using sweet potatoes instead of white ones for an alternative curry with a sweeter flavour.

Masala Okra

Okra or 'ladies' fingers' are a popular Indian vegetable. In this recipe they are stir-fried with a dry, spicy masala to make a delicious side dish.

Serves 4

2.5ml/½ tsp ground turmeric
5ml/1 tsp chilli powder
15ml/1 tbsp ground cumin
15ml/1 tbsp ground coriander
1.5ml/¼ tsp salt
1.5ml/¼ tsp sugar
15ml/1 tbsp lemon juice
15ml/1 tbsp desiccated (dry unsweetened shredded) coconut
30ml/2 tbsp chopped fresh coriander (cilantro)
45ml/3 tbsp oil
2.5ml/½ tsp cumin seeds
2.5ml/½ tsp black mustard seeds
450g/1lb okra, washed and trimmed
chopped fresh tomatoes, to garnish
poppadums, to serve

3 Add the spice mixture to the pan and continue to fry for 2 minutes, stirring frequently to prevent the spices from burning on the bottom of the pan.

4 Add the okra, cover, and cook over a low heat for 10 minutes, or until tender. Garnish with chopped fresh tomatoes and serve with poppadums.

1 Combine the turmeric, chilli powder, cumin, ground coriander, salt, sugar, lemon juice, coconut and fresh coriander.

2 Heat the oil in a large frying pan. Add the cumin seeds and mustard seeds and fry for about 2 minutes, until they splutter.

Mixed Vegetable Curry

This is a good all-round vegetable curry that goes well with most Indian meat dishes. You can use any combination of vegetables that are in season.

Serves 4

30ml/2 tbsp oil
2.5ml/½ tsp black mustard seeds
2.5ml/½ tsp cumin seeds
1 onion, peeled and thinly sliced
2 curry leaves
1 green chilli, finely chopped
2.5cm/1in piece root ginger, peeled and finely chopped
30ml/2 tbsp curry paste
1 small cauliflower, broken into florets
1 large carrot, peeled and thickly sliced into rounds
115g/4oz French (green) beans, cut into 2.5cm/1in lengths
1.5ml/¼ tsp ground turmeric
1.5ml/¼ tsp chilli powder
2.5ml/½ tsp salt
2 tomatoes, finely chopped
50g/2oz frozen peas, thawed
150ml/¼ pint/⅔ cup vegetable stock
fresh curry leaves, to garnish

1 Heat the oil in a large pan and fry the mustard seeds and cumin seeds for 2 minutes, until they begin to splutter.

2 Add the sliced onion and the curry leaves to the pan and fry for 5 minutes, stirring frequently, until the onion is starting to soften.

3 Add the finely chopped chilli and ginger to the pan and fry for 2 minutes. Stir in the curry paste and fry for 3–4 minutes, stirring frequently to prevent the mixture from sticking.

4 Add the cauliflower florets, carrot and French beans to the pan, stir to combine, and cook for 4–5 minutes. Add the ground turmeric, chilli powder, salt and finely chopped tomatoes and cook for 2–3 minutes, stirring occasionally.

5 Add the thawed peas and cook for a further 2–3 minutes.

6 Add the stock. Cover and simmer over a low heat for 10–15 minutes until all the vegetables are tender. Serve, garnished with curry leaves.

Banana Curry

The sweetness of bananas combines well with the spices, producing a mild, sweet curry. Choose ones that are slightly under-ripe so that they retain their shape and do not become mushy.

Serves 4

4 under-ripe bananas
30ml/2 tbsp ground coriander
15ml/1 tbsp ground cumin
5ml/1 tsp chilli powder
2.5ml/½ tsp salt
1.5ml/¼ tsp ground turmeric
5ml/1 tsp sugar
15ml/1 tbsp gram flour
45ml/3 tbsp chopped fresh coriander
    (cilantro), plus sprigs, to garnish
90ml/6 tbsp oil
1.5ml/¼ tsp cumin seeds
1.5ml/¼ tsp black mustard seeds
chapatis, to serve

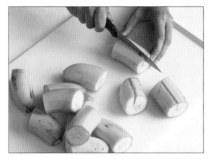

1 Trim off the ends of the bananas, then cut each into three equal pieces, leaving the skin on. Make a deep lengthways slit in each piece of banana, without cutting all the way through.

2 On a plate, mix together the coriander, cumin, chilli powder, salt, turmeric, sugar, gram flour, fresh coriander and 15ml/1 tbsp of the oil.

3 Carefully stuff each piece of banana with the spice mixture, taking care not to break them in half.

4 Heat the remaining oil in a large, heavy pan and fry the cumin and mustard seeds for 2 minutes or until they splutter. Add the bananas and toss gently in the oil. Cover and simmer over a low heat for 15 minutes, stirring until the bananas are soft, but not mushy. Garnish with fresh coriander and serve with warm chapatis.

Aubergine Curry

This is a simple and delicious way of cooking aubergines or eggplants that retains their full flavour. The curry is substantial enough to be a meal on its own.

Serves 4

2 large aubergines (eggplants)
45ml/3 tbsp oil
2.5ml/½ tsp black mustard seeds
115g/4oz button (white) mushrooms
1 bunch spring onions (scallions), chopped
2 garlic cloves, peeled and crushed
1 red chilli, finely chopped
2.5ml/½ tsp chilli powder
5ml/1 tsp ground cumin
5ml/1 tsp ground coriander
1.5ml/¼ tsp ground turmeric
5ml/1 tsp salt
400g/14oz can chopped tomatoes
15ml/1 tbsp chopped fresh coriander
    (cilantro), plus a sprig, to garnish

1 Preheat the oven to 200°C/400°F/Gas 6. Brush both of the aubergines with 15ml/ 1 tbsp of the oil and prick with a fork. Bake for 30–35 minutes until the aubergines are soft.

2 Meanwhile, heat the remaining oil in a pan. Fry the mustard seeds for 2 minutes, until they begin to splutter. Halve the mushrooms and add them with the onions, garlic and chilli and fry for 5 minutes. Stir in the chilli powder, cumin, coriander, turmeric and salt. Fry for 4 minutes. Add the tomatoes and simmer for 5 minutes.

COOK'S TIP

If you want to omit the oil, you can wrap the aubergines (eggplants) in foil and bake in the oven for 1 hour.

3 Carefully cut each of the aubergines in half lengthways (they will be hot) and scoop out the soft flesh into a bowl. Mash the flesh briefly with a fork or spoon until it is quite smooth.

4 Add the mashed aubergine and fresh coriander to the pan. Bring to the boil and simmer for 5 minutes or until the sauce thickens. Serve, garnished with a fresh coriander sprig.

Corn and Pea Curry

In this simple dish, tender corn is cooked in a spicy tomato sauce along with vibrant fresh peas. Use fresh corn when it is in season, or thawed frozen corn when the fresh type is not available.

Serves 4

6 pieces of frozen corn on the cob
45ml/3 tbsp oil
2.5ml/½ tsp cumin seeds
1 onion, peeled and finely chopped
2 garlic cloves, peeled and crushed
1 green chilli, finely chopped
15ml/1 tbsp curry paste
5ml/1 tsp ground coriander
5ml/1 tsp ground cumin
1.5ml/¼ tsp ground turmeric
2.5ml/½ tsp salt
2.5ml/½ tsp sugar
400g/14oz can chopped tomatoes
15ml/1 tbsp tomato purée (paste)
150ml/¼ pint/⅔ cup water
115g/4oz frozen peas, thawed
30ml/2 tbsp chopped fresh
    coriander (cilantro)
chapatis, to serve (optional)

1 Cut each piece of corn in half to make 12 equal pieces in total. Bring a large pan of water to the boil and cook the corn on the cob pieces for 10–12 minutes, until tender. Drain well.

2 Heat the oil in large pan and fry the cumin seeds for 2 minutes or until they begin to splutter. Add the onion, garlic and chilli and fry for about 10 minutes, stirring frequently, until the onions are golden and softened.

3 Add the curry paste and fry, stirring frequently, for 2 minutes. Stir in the remaining spices, salt and sugar and fry for 2–3 minutes.

VARIATION
If you don't like peas then you can replace them with the same quantity of frozen corn, if you prefer.

4 Add the chopped tomatoes and tomato purée to the pan together with the water and simmer for about 5 minutes or until the sauce thickens, stirring frequently to prevent the mixture from sticking. Stir in the thawed peas and cook for a further 5 minutes.

5 Add the pieces of cooked corn on the cob pieces and the fresh coriander to the pan and cook for a further 2 minutes or until the corn is heated through.

6 Serve the curry with chapatis, for mopping up the rich sauce and making the meal more substantial, if you like.

Aloo Saag

Spinach, potatoes and traditional Indian spices are the main ingredients in this simple, delicious and authentic curry, which makes a healthy meal.

Serves 4

450g/1lb spinach
30ml/2 tbsp oil
5ml/1 tsp black mustard seeds
1 onion, peeled and thinly sliced
2 garlic cloves, peeled and crushed
2.5cm/1in piece root ginger, peeled and finely chopped
675g/1½lb potatoes, peeled and cut into 2.5cm/1in chunks
5ml/1 tsp chilli powder
5ml/1 tsp salt
120ml/4fl oz/½ cup water

3 Heat the oil in a large pan and fry the mustard seeds for 2 minutes or until they begin to splutter.

5 Add the potatoes, chilli powder, salt and water and cook for 8 minutes.

1 Wash the spinach, then blanch it in boiling water for 1–2 minutes.

2 Drain the spinach thoroughly and set it aside. When it is cool enough to handle, use your hands to squeeze out any remaining liquid.

COOK'S TIP

To make certain the spinach is dry, put it in a clean dish towel, roll it up tightly and squeeze to remove any excess liquid.

4 Add the onion, garlic and ginger and fry for 5 minutes, stirring.

6 Add the spinach to the pan. Cover and simmer for 10–15 minutes or until the potatoes are tender. Serve hot.

COOK'S TIPS

Use a waxy rather than a floury variety of potato for this dish so the pieces do not break up during cooking.

VARIATION

To add protein to the dish, you could include some cubed paneer (Indian cheese), or some toasted cashew nuts.

Mushroom Curry

This is a tasty way of cooking mushrooms, melding their natural earthy flavour with aromatic spices. It goes well with most meat dishes.

Serves 4

30ml/2 tbsp oil
2.5ml/½ tsp cumin seeds
1.5ml/¼ tsp black peppercorns
4 green cardamom pods
1.5ml/¼ tsp ground turmeric
1 onion, peeled and finely chopped
5ml/1 tsp ground cumin
5ml/1 tsp ground coriander
2.5ml/½ tsp garam masala
1 green chilli, finely chopped
2 garlic cloves, peeled and crushed
2.5cm/1in piece root ginger, peeled
   and grated
400g/14oz can chopped tomatoes
1.5ml/¼ tsp salt
450g/1lb button (white)
   mushrooms, halved
chopped fresh coriander (cilantro),
   to garnish

1 Heat the oil in a pan and fry the cumin, peppercorns, cardamoms and turmeric for 2–3 minutes. Add the onion and fry for 5 minutes. Stir in the cumin, coriander and garam masala. Fry for 2 minutes.

2 Add the chilli, garlic and ginger and fry for 2–3 minutes, stirring all the time to prevent the spices from sticking to the pan. Add the tomatoes and salt. Bring to the boil and simmer for 5 minutes.

3 Add the mushrooms. Cover and simmer over a low heat for 10 minutes. Garnish with chopped fresh coriander. This curry would be good with Spicy Lamb and Potato Stew (see pages 32–3).

Spicy Bitter Gourds

Bitter gourds are widely used in Indian cooking, both on their own and combined with other vegetables in a curry, as in this dish.

Serves 4

675g/1½lb bitter gourds
60ml/4 tbsp oil
2.5ml/½ tsp cumin seeds
6 spring onions (scallions), finely chopped
5 tomatoes, finely chopped
2.5cm/1in piece root ginger, peeled
   and finely chopped
2 garlic cloves, peeled and crushed
2 green chillies, finely chopped
2.5ml/½ tsp salt
2.5ml/½ tsp chilli powder
5ml/1 tsp ground coriander
5ml/1 tsp ground cumin
45ml/3 tbsp peanuts, crushed
45ml/3 tbsp soft dark brown sugar
15ml/1 tbsp gram flour
fresh coriander (cilantro) sprigs, to garnish

1 Bring a large pan of lightly salted water to the boil. Peel the bitter gourds using a small sharp knife and halve them. Discard the seeds. Cut into 2cm/¾in pieces, then cook in the water for 10–15 minutes, until tender. Drain well and set aside.

2 Heat the oil in a large pan and fry the cumin seeds for 2 minutes, until they begin to splutter. Add the spring onions and fry for 3–4 minutes. Add the tomatoes, ginger, garlic and chillies and cook for 5 minutes.

COOK'S TIP
Crush the peanuts by processing them for 20–30 seconds in a food processor.

3 Add the salt, remaining spices, the crushed peanuts and the brown sugar to the pan and cook for about 2–3 minutes, stirring occasionally. Add the bitter gourds and mix well.

4 Sprinkle over the gram flour. Cover and simmer over a low heat for 5–8 minutes or until all of the gram flour has been absorbed. Serve garnished with fresh coriander sprigs.

Spicy Potatoes with Sesame Seeds

This recipe is a variation of the well-known dish Bombay Potatoes, in which the potatoes are fried to give them a crispy texture, then tossed in spices and sesame seeds.

Serves 4

900g/2lb potatoes, peeled
oil, for deep-frying
1.5ml/¼ tsp ground turmeric
1.5ml/¼ tsp chilli powder
1.5ml/¼ tsp salt
30ml/2 tbsp oil
1.5ml/¼ tsp black mustard seeds
1 green chilli, finely chopped
1 garlic clove, peeled and crushed
30ml/2 tbsp sesame seeds

1 Cut the potatoes into thick chips or fries. Heat the oil for deep-frying in a suitable pan to 160°C/325°F. Alternatively, use a deep-fat fryer if you have one.

2 Fry the chips in batches for 5 minutes, until golden and crispy. Lift them out using a slotted spoon and drain well on plenty of kitchen paper.

COOK'S TIP
Make sure the chips or fries are as uniform in size as possible to ensure that they cook evenly.

3 Put the chips in a bowl and sprinkle over the turmeric, chilli powder and salt. Cool, then toss the chips in the spices until they are evenly coated.

4 Heat the 30ml/2 tbsp oil in a large pan and fry the mustard seeds for 2 minutes until they splutter. Add the chilli and garlic and fry for 2 minutes.

5 Add the sesame seeds to the pan and fry for 3–4 minutes, until the seeds begin to brown, stirring frequently to prevent the seeds from burning. Remove the pan from the heat.

6 Add the sesame seed mixture to the potatoes in the bowl and toss together to coat the chips evenly.

7 Serve the chips cold, or reheat them on a baking sheet for 5 minutes in an oven preheated to 200°C/400°F/Gas 6. Do not leave them in the oven for longer than this or the sesame seed crust could burn and taste bitter.

Courgette Curry

Thickly sliced courgettes or zucchini are combined with authentic Indian spices for this colourful vegetable curry. You could use aubergines or eggplants instead of courgettes, if you like.

Serves 4

675g/1½lb courgettes (zucchini)
45ml/3 tbsp oil
2.5ml/½ tsp cumin seeds
2.5ml/½ tsp mustard seeds
1 onion, peeled and thinly sliced
2 garlic cloves, peeled and crushed
1.5ml/¼ tsp ground turmeric
1.5ml/¼ tsp chilli powder
5ml/1 tsp ground coriander
5ml/1 tsp ground cumin
2.5ml/½ tsp salt
15ml/1 tbsp tomato purée (paste)
400g/14oz can chopped tomatoes
150ml/¼ pint/⅔ cup water
15ml/1 tbsp chopped fresh
    coriander (cilantro)
5ml/1 tsp garam masala

1 Trim the ends from the courgettes, then cut them into 1cm/½in-thick slices.

2 Heat the oil in a large pan and fry the cumin seeds and mustard seeds for about 2 minutes, until they begin to splutter, stirring frequently.

3 Add the onion and garlic and fry for about 5–6 minutes.

4 Add the ground turmeric, chilli powder, ground coriander, ground cumin and salt and fry for about 2–3 minutes.

5 Add the sliced courgettes to the pan all at once, and cook for 2 minutes, stirring once or twice.

6 Mix together the tomato purée and chopped tomatoes and add the mixture to the pan along with the water. Stir to combine thoroughly, then simmer for 5 minutes, until the sauce thickens and reduces slightly.

7 Gently stir in the fresh coriander and the garam masala, taking care not to break up the courgettes, then cook for about 2 minutes or until the courgettes are just tender.

Vegetable Kashmiri

This is a delicious vegetable curry, in which fresh mixed vegetables are cooked in a spicy, aromatic yogurt sauce and garnished with toasted almonds.

Serves 4

10ml/2 tsp cumin seeds
8 black peppercorns
2 green cardamom pods, seeds only
5cm/2in cinnamon stick
2.5ml/½ tsp grated nutmeg
45ml/3 tbsp oil
1 green chilli, chopped
2.5cm/1in piece root ginger, peeled and grated
5ml/1 tsp chilli powder
2.5ml/½ tsp salt
2 large potatoes, peeled and cut into 2.5cm/1in chunks
225g/8oz cauliflower, broken into small florets
225g/8oz okra, thickly sliced
150ml/¼ pint/⅔ cup natural (plain) yogurt
150ml/¼ pint/⅔ cup vegetable stock
toasted flaked (sliced) almonds and fresh coriander (cilantro) sprigs, to garnish

1 Grind the cumin seeds, peppercorns, cardamom seeds, cinnamon stick and nutmeg to a fine powder using a blender or a pestle and mortar.

2 Heat the oil in a large pan and fry the chilli and ginger for 2 minutes, stirring all the time.

3 Add the chilli powder, salt and ground spice mixture and fry for 2–3 minutes, stirring all the time to prevent the spices from sticking.

4 Stir in the potatoes, cover the pan, and cook for 10 minutes over a low heat, stirring from time to time.

VARIATION
You can mix and match vegetables in this dish. Butternut squash, broccoli or green beans would all work well.

5 Add the cauliflower and okra and cook for 5 minutes.

6 Add the yogurt and stock. Bring to the boil, then reduce the heat. Cover and simmer for 20 minutes, or until all the vegetables are tender.

7 Garnish with toasted almonds and fresh coriander sprigs and serve.

Stuffed Baby Vegetables

The combination of potatoes and aubergines or eggplants is popular in Indian cooking. This recipe uses baby vegetables, which are stuffed with a dry, spicy masala paste.

Serves 4

12 small potatoes
8 baby aubergines (eggplants)

For the stuffing
15ml/1 tbsp sesame seeds
30ml/2 tbsp ground coriander
30ml/2 tbsp ground cumin
2.5ml/½ tsp salt
1.5ml/¼ tsp chilli powder
2.5ml/½ tsp ground turmeric
10ml/2 tsp sugar
1.5ml/¼ tsp garam masala
15ml/1 tbsp peanuts, roughly crushed
15ml/1 tbsp gram flour
2 garlic cloves, peeled and crushed
15ml/1 tbsp lemon juice
30ml/2 tbsp chopped fresh
    coriander (cilantro)

For the sauce
30ml/2 tbsp oil
2.5ml/½ tsp black mustard seeds
400g/14oz can chopped tomatoes
30ml/2 tbsp chopped fresh coriander
    (cilantro)
150ml/¼ pint/⅔ cup water
single (light) cream, to garnish (optional)

1 Preheat the oven to 200°C/400°F/
Gas 6.

2 Peel the potatoes, then make deep slits in both them and the aubergines, making sure that you do not cut right through. Open out the vegetables slightly.

3 Mix together all the ingredients for the stuffing on a plate.

4 Carefully stuff the opened-out slits in the potatoes and aubergines with the spice mixture. Place the vegetables in a greased ovenproof dish.

5 Heat the oil in a pan and fry the mustard seeds for 2 minutes, until they begin to splutter, then add the tomatoes, coriander and any leftover stuffing together with the water. Simmer for 5 minutes, until the sauce thickens.

6 Pour the tomato sauce over the potatoes and aubergines in the dish. Cover and bake for 25–30 minutes, until the potatoes and aubergines are soft when tested with a fork or the tip of a sharp knife.

7 Garnish with single cream, if using, and serve immediately.

Chicken Biryani

Biryanis originated in Persia, and are traditionally made with meat and rice. They are often served at dinner parties and on festive occasions.

Serves 4

275g/10oz/1½ cups basmati rice
30ml/2 tbsp oil
1 onion, peeled and thinly sliced
2 garlic cloves, peeled and crushed
1 green chilli, finely chopped
2.5cm/1in piece root ginger, peeled
   and finely chopped
675g/1½lb chicken breast fillets, skinned
   and cut into 2.5cm/1in cubes
45ml/3 tbsp curry paste
1.5ml/¼ tsp salt
1.5ml/¼ tsp garam masala
3 tomatoes, cut into thin wedges
1.5ml/¼ tsp ground turmeric
2 bay leaves
4 green cardamom pods
4 cloves
1.5ml/¼ tsp saffron strands
Tomato and Chilli Chutney (see page 20),
   to serve

1 Wash the basmati rice in a strainer under cold running water, until the water runs clear. Transfer to a bowl, cover with plenty of water and leave to soak for 30 minutes.

2 Meanwhile, heat the oil in a large frying pan and fry the onion for 5–7 minutes, until lightly browned. Add the garlic, green chilli and ginger and stir-fry for about 2 minutes.

3 Add the cubed chicken pieces to the frying pan and fry for 5 minutes, stirring occasionally, until browned all over.

4 Add the curry paste, salt and garam masala to the pan and cook for 5 minutes, stirring occasionally. Add the tomatoes and continue to cook for 3–4 minutes, stirring occasionally. Remove from the heat and set aside.

5 Preheat the oven to 190°C/375°F/ Gas 5. Bring a large pan of water to the boil. Drain the soaked rice and add it to the pan with the turmeric. Cook for about 10 minutes, or until the rice is almost tender. Drain the rice and toss it together with the bay leaves, cardamoms, cloves and saffron in a bowl.

6 Layer the rice and chicken in a shallow, ovenproof dish until all the mixture has been used, finishing off with a layer of rice. Cover and bake for 15–20 minutes, or until the chicken is tender. Serve with Tomato and Chilli Chutney.

Kidney Bean Curry

This a very popular Punjabi-style dish using red kidney beans, but you can substitute the same quantity of butter beans or lima beans, if you prefer.

Serves 4

225g/8oz dried red kidney beans
30ml/2 tbsp oil
2.5ml/½ tsp cumin seeds
1 onion, peeled and thinly sliced
1 green chilli, finely chopped
2 garlic cloves, peeled and crushed
2.5cm/1in piece root ginger, peeled
    and grated
30ml/2 tbsp curry paste
5ml/1 tsp ground cumin
5ml/1 tsp ground coriander
2.5ml/½ tsp chilli powder
2.5ml/½ tsp salt
400g/14oz can chopped tomatoes
30ml/2 tbsp chopped fresh coriander
    (cilantro), to garnish

1 Place the kidney beans in a large bowl of cold water, then cover with clear film (plastic wrap) and leave them to soak at room temperature overnight. This soaking process is very important, as kidney beans can be toxic, so do not be tempted to skip this step.

2 Drain the beans and place in a large pan with double the volume of water. Boil for 10 minutes. Skim off any scum. Cover and cook for 1–1½ hours, until soft.

3 Meanwhile, heat the oil in a large frying pan and fry the cumin seeds for 2 minutes until they splutter. Add the onion, chilli, garlic and ginger and fry for 5 minutes. Stir in the curry paste, cumin, coriander, chilli powder and salt. Cook for 5 minutes.

4 Add the tomatoes. Simmer for 5 minutes. Add the beans and coriander, reserving some for the garnish. Cover and cook for 15 minutes, adding water if necessary. Serve, garnished with coriander.

Spinach Dhal

There are many types of dhals eaten in India, each region having its own speciality. This is a lightly spiced dish with a mild nutty flavour from the lentils, which combines well with the spinach.

Serves 4

175g/6oz/1 cup chana dhal or
    yellow split peas
175ml/6fl oz/¾ cup water
30ml/2 tbsp oil
1.5ml/¼ tsp black mustard seeds
1 onion, peeled and thinly sliced
2 garlic cloves, peeled and crushed
2.5cm/1in piece root ginger, peeled
    and grated
1 red chilli, finely chopped
275g/10oz frozen spinach, thawed
1.5ml/¼ tsp chilli powder
2.5ml/½ tsp ground coriander
2.5ml/½ tsp garam masala
2.5ml/½ tsp salt

1 Wash the chana dhal or split peas in a strainer under cold running water, until the water runs clear. Transfer the dhal or peas to a large bowl and cover with plenty of water. Cover and leave to soak for 30 minutes.

2 Drain the chana dhal or split peas and put in a large pan with the water. Bring to the boil, cover and simmer for 25 minutes.

3 Meanwhile, heat the oil in a large frying pan. Fry the mustard seeds for 2 minutes, until they splutter. Add the onion, garlic, ginger and chilli and fry for 5–6 minutes. Add the spinach and cook for 5 minutes or until the spinach is dry and the liquid has been absorbed. Stir in the remaining spices and salt and cook for 2–3 minutes.

4 Drain the chana dhal or split peas, add to the spinach and cook for about 5 minutes, until heated through. Transfer to a dish and serve immediately.

Masala Chana

Chickpeas are used and cooked in a variety of ways all over the Indian sub-continent. Tamarind gives this dish a deliciously sharp, tangy flavour and vibrant colour.

Serves 4

225g/8oz/1¼ cups dried chickpeas
50g/2oz tamarind pulp
120ml/4fl oz/½ cup boiling water
45ml/3 tbsp oil
2.5ml/½ tsp cumin seeds
1 onion, peeled and finely chopped
2 garlic cloves, peeled and crushed
2.5cm/1in piece root ginger, peeled and grated
1 green chilli, seeded (optional) and finely chopped
5ml/1 tsp ground cumin
5ml/1 tsp ground coriander
1.5ml/¼ tsp ground turmeric
2.5ml/½ tsp salt
225g/8oz tomatoes, skinned and finely chopped
2.5ml/½ tsp garam masala
chopped chillies and chopped onion, to garnish

2 Drain the chickpeas and place them in a large pan with double the volume of cold water. Bring to the boil and boil vigorously for 10 minutes. Skim off any scum. Cover and simmer for 1½–2 hours or until the chickpeas are soft.

3 Meanwhile, break up the tamarind and soak it in a bowl in the boiling water for about 15 minutes. Rub the tamarind pulp through a strainer into a bowl, discarding any stones and fibre.

5 Add the cumin, coriander, turmeric and salt and fry for 3–4 minutes. Add the tomatoes and tamarind pulp. Bring to the boil and simmer for 5 minutes.

6 Add the chickpeas and garam masala to the pan. Cover and simmer for about 15 minutes. Garnish with chopped chillies and onion.

COOK'S TIP
To save time, make double the quantity of tamarind pulp and freeze it in ice-cube trays. It will keep for up to 2 months. Alternatively, you can buy tamarind paste or concentrate and use that instead.

1 Put the chickpeas in a large bowl and cover them with plenty of cold water. Cover with clear film (plastic wrap) and leave to soak overnight.

4 Heat the oil in a large pan and fry the cumin seeds for 2 minutes, until they splutter. Add the onion, garlic, ginger and chilli and fry for 5 minutes.

Lentils and Rice

Lentils are cooked with whole and ground spices, potatoes, rice and onions in this dish to produce an authentic Indian-style risotto.

Serves 4

150g/5oz/¾ cup toovar dhal or
    red split lentils
115g/4oz/generous ½ cup basmati rice
1 large potato
1 large onion
30ml/2 tbsp oil
4 whole cloves
1.5ml/¼ tsp cumin seeds
1.5ml/¼ tsp ground turmeric
10ml/2 tsp salt
300ml/½ pints/1¼ cups water

3 Peel and then thinly slice the onion.

5 Add the onion and potatoes to the heavy pan and fry for 5 minutes, stirring occasionally, until the onion starts to soften. Add the lentils, rice, turmeric and salt to the pan and fry for 3 minutes, stirring frequently.

1 Wash the toovar dhal or lentils and rice in a strainer under cold running water, until the water runs clear. Transfer to a bowl and cover with water. Leave to soak for 15 minutes, then drain.

2 Peel the potato, then cut it into roughly even 2.5cm/1in chunks.

VARIATION
You could add some vegetables to this dish. Finely chopped (bell) pepper, sliced mushrooms or peas would work well.

4 Heat the oil in a large, heavy pan and fry the cloves and cumin seeds for about 2 minutes, until the seeds are beginning to splutter.

6 Add the water. Bring to the boil, cover and simmer for 15–20 minutes, until all the water has been absorbed and the potatoes are tender.

7 Leave the mixture to stand, keeping the pan covered, for about 10 minutes before fluffing up the rice with a fork and then serving immediately.

Mung Beans with Potatoes

One of the quicker-cooking pulses, mung beans do not require soaking. In this recipe they are cooked with potatoes and traditional Indian spices to produce a tasty, nutritious dish.

Serves 4

175g/6oz/1 cup mung beans
750ml/1¼ pints/3 cups water
225g/8oz potatoes, peeled and cut into
    2cm/¾in chunks
30ml/2 tbsp oil
2.5ml/½ tsp cumin seeds
1 green chilli, finely chopped
1 garlic clove, peeled and crushed
2.5cm/1in piece root ginger, peeled
    and finely chopped
1.5ml/¼ tsp ground turmeric
2.5ml/½ tsp chilli powder
5ml/1 tsp salt
5ml/1 tsp sugar
4 curry leaves
5 tomatoes, skinned and finely chopped
15ml/1 tbsp tomato purée (paste)
curry leaves, to garnish
plain rice, to serve

1 Wash the mung beans. Bring to the boil in the water, cover and simmer for about 30 minutes, until soft. Par-boil the potatoes for 10 minutes in another pan, then drain them well.

2 Heat the oil and fry the cumin seeds until they splutter. Add the chilli, garlic and ginger and fry for 3–4 minutes.

3 Add the ground turmeric, chilli powder, salt and sugar to the pan and cook for about 2 minutes, stirring constantly to prevent the mixture from sticking to the pan and burning.

4 Add the curry leaves, tomatoes and tomato purée and simmer for 5 minutes until the sauce thickens. Combine the sauce, potatoes and mung beans. Serve with rice, and garnish with curry leaves.

Madras Sambal

This dish is regularly cooked in one form or another in almost every south-Indian home and served as part of a meal. You can use any combination of vegetables that are in season.

Serves 4

225g/8oz/1 cup toovar dhal or
    red split lentils
600ml/1 pint/2½ cups water
2.5ml/½ tsp ground turmeric
2 large potatoes, peeled and cut into
    2.5cm/1in chunks
30ml/2 tbsp oil
2.5ml/½ tsp black mustard seeds
1.5ml/¼ tsp fenugreek seeds
4 curry leaves
1 onion, peeled and thinly sliced
115g/4oz French (green) beans, cut into
    2.5cm/1in lengths
5ml/1 tsp salt
2.5ml/½ tsp chilli powder
15ml/1 tbsp lemon juice
60ml/4 tbsp desiccated (dry unsweetened
    shredded) coconut
toasted coconut, to garnish
Fresh Coriander Chutney (see page 21),
    to serve

1 Thoroughly wash the toovar dhal or lentils in several changes of water. Place them in a heavy pan with the water and the turmeric. Cover and simmer for 30–35 minutes, until the lentils are soft.

2 Par-boil the potatoes in a large pan of boiling water for 10 minutes. Drain well and set aside.

3 Heat the oil in a large frying pan and fry the mustard seeds, fenugreek seeds and curry leaves for 2–3 minutes, until the seeds splutter. Add the onion and the French beans and fry for 7–8 minutes. Add the potatoes and cook for a further 2 minutes.

4 Stir in the the lentils with the salt, chilli powder and lemon juice and simmer for 2 minutes. Stir in the coconut and simmer for 5 minutes. Garnish with toasted coconut and serve with Fresh Coriander Chutney.

Mixed Bean Curry

You can use any combination of dried beans that you have in the storecupboard or pantry for this recipe. It can be made in advance and reheated.

Serves 4

50g/2oz/⅓ cup red kidney beans
50g/2oz/⅓ cup black-eyed
    (pinto) beans
50g/2oz/⅓ cup haricot (navy) beans
50g/2oz/⅓ cup flageolet (small
    cannellini) beans
30ml/2 tbsp oil
5ml/1 tsp cumin seeds
5ml/1 tsp black mustard seeds
1 onion, peeled and finely chopped
2 garlic cloves, peeled and crushed
2.5cm/1in piece root ginger, peeled
    and grated
2 green chillies, finely chopped
30ml/2 tbsp curry paste
2.5ml/½ tsp salt
400g/14oz can chopped tomatoes
30ml/2 tbsp tomato purée (paste)
250ml/8fl oz/1 cup water
30ml/2 tbsp chopped fresh coriander
    (cilantro), plus extra, to garnish

1 Put the beans in a large bowl and cover with plenty of cold water. Leave to soak overnight, stirring occasionally.

2 Drain the beans and transfer them to a large, heavy pan with double the volume of cold water. Boil the beans vigorously for 10 minutes. Skim off any scum. Cover and simmer for 1½ hours or until the beans are soft.

3 Heat the oil in a large pan and fry the cumin seeds and mustard seeds for about 2 minutes, until the seeds begin to splutter. Add the onion, garlic, ginger and chilli and fry for 5 minutes, stirring occasionally, until the onion starts to soften.

4 Add the curry paste to the pan and fry for a further 2–3 minutes, stirring, then add the salt.

5 Add the tomatoes, tomato purée and the water to the pan and simmer for 5 minutes.

6 Add the drained beans and the fresh coriander. Cover and simmer for about 30–40 minutes, until the sauce thickens and the beans are cooked.

7 Garnish with chopped fresh coriander and serve.

COOK'S TIP
Depending on the types of beans you use, you may need to adjust the cooking time; they should be tender once cooked.

Egg and Lentil Curry

A few Indian spices can transform eggs and lentils into a tasty, economical curry that makes a nutritious and colourful meal-in-a-bowl.

Serves 4

75g/3oz/⅓ cup green lentils
750ml/1¼ pints/3 cups vegetable stock
6 eggs
30ml/2 tbsp oil
3 cloves
1.5ml/¼ tsp black peppercorns
1 onion, peeled and finely chopped
2 green chillies, finely chopped
2 garlic cloves, peeled and crushed
2.5cm/1in root ginger, peeled and chopped
30ml/2 tbsp curry paste
400g/14oz can chopped tomatoes
2.5ml/½ tsp sugar
2.5ml/½ tsp garam masala

1 Wash the lentils under cold running water, checking for small stones. Put in a large, heavy pan with the stock. Cover and simmer gently for about 15 minutes or until the lentils are soft. Drain the lentils and set aside.

2 Cook the eggs in a pan of boiling water for 10 minutes. When cool enough to handle, peel and cut in half lengthways.

3 Heat the oil in a large pan and fry the cloves and black peppercorns for about 2 minutes. Add the onion, chillies, garlic and ginger and fry the mixture for a further 5–6 minutes.

4 Stir in the curry paste and fry for about 2 minutes, stirring frequently.

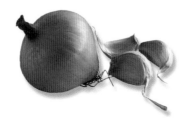

5 Stir in the tomatoes and sugar with 175ml/6fl oz/¾ cup water.

6 Simmer for 5 minutes, until the sauce thickens. Add the halved hard-boiled eggs, drained lentils and garam masala to the pan and stir gently without breaking up the eggs. Cover and simmer for about 10 minutes, then serve immediately.

COOK'S TIP
Do not cook the eggs in the sauce for much longer than about 10 minutes or they will become rubbery in texture. For the same reason, the dish should be served immediately.

Vegetable Pilau

This is a popular vegetable rice dish that goes well with most Indian meat dishes, or can be enjoyed on its own as a tasty vegetarian main course.

Serves 4–6

225g/8oz/1 cup basmati rice
30ml/2 tbsp oil
2.5ml/½ tsp cumin seeds
2 bay leaves
4 green cardamom pods
4 cloves
1 onion, peeled and finely chopped
1 carrot, peeled and finely diced
50g/2oz/½ cup frozen peas, thawed
50g/2oz/⅓ cup frozen corn, thawed
25g/1oz/¼ cup cashew nuts, lightly fried
475ml/16fl oz/2 cups water
1.5ml/¼ tsp ground cumin
1.5ml/¼ tsp ground coriander
2.5ml/½ tsp salt

1 Wash the basmati rice in several changes of cold water. Transfer to a bowl and cover with water. Leave to soak for 30 minutes.

2 Heat the oil in a large frying pan and fry the cumin seeds for 2 minutes. Add the bay leaves, cardamoms and cloves and fry for 2 minutes.

3 Add the onion and fry for 5 minutes, until lightly browned.

4 Stir in the chopped carrot and cook for 3–4 minutes, stirring frequently.

5 Drain the rice and add it to the pan with the peas, corn and cashew nuts. Fry for 4–5 minutes.

6 Add the water, remaining spices and salt to the pan. Bring to the boil, cover, and simmer for 15 minutes over a low heat until all the water is absorbed.

7 Leave the mixture to stand, covered, for 10 minutes before fluffing up the rice with a fork and serving.

VARIATION
Thawed frozen mixed vegetables would be ideal in this dish, for speed.

Index